"Mick Mica's book, *Not Quite Finished*, is a rewarding read. It causes the reader to feel as if they are living inside a spiritual travel guide. The reader vividly experiences each step of the journey as the Mica family follows the Lord's leadership to serve among nations, tribes, and various people groups. We experience through these pages all types landscapes, and we can almost feel beneath their feet the rocks, compacted earth, and steep hills and mountains to be traversed through the author's recounting of each challenge and lesson learned. I recommend this book without reservation. May it inspire many to undertake their own personal journeys as they cross the street *or* the ocean and view life as a never-ending adventure."

—**Dr. Nik Ripken**
Author of *The Insanity of God*

"If you are considering going into Christian missions, you will want to read this. If you just like great stories, you will want to read this. Told with sometimes brazen honesty, this book carries you to forgotten lands and people where God is working."

—**Jeffrey Deal**
Author of *The Mark, Toccoa,* and *The Rhythm of Grace on Standalone Mountain*

"Very few times in life do Christ followers have the opportunity to observe or read about what a surrendered life really looks like. In reading this life story of two 'called ones,' the passion of their lives was to respond to Him in the darkest of places—and this is where they found Him. Simply becoming Him among them."

—**Dwight Bass**
A colleague who served faithfully for twenty-nine years on the field

"I loved this book. I've known Mick and Kate for three decades, and I've walked in many of their same paths. What a blessed adventure their lives have been! Can't wait to put this book into the hands of my grown missionary children and friends."

—**David Garrison**
Missionary Author, *Church Planting Movements*

NOT QUITE FINISHED

GOD'S WORK THROUGH HIS SERVANTS

Mick Mica

Published by Innovo Publishing, LLC
www.innovopublishing.com
1-888-546-2111

Publishing quality books, eBooks, audiobooks, music, screenplays & courses for the Christian & wholesome markets since 2008.

NOT QUITE FINISHED
God's Work Through His Servants

Copyright © 2024 by Mick Mica
All rights reserved.

*Many of the names in this book have been changed for the security and safety of individuals involved. All names that include an asterisk are pseudonyms.

No part of this publication may be reproduced, stored in a retrieval system, or transmitted in any form or by any means electronic, mechanical, photocopying, recording, or otherwise, without the prior written permission of the Author.

Unless otherwise noted, all scripture is from the Holy Bible, New Living Translation, copyright © 1996, 2004, 2015 by Tyndale House Foundation. Used by permission of Tyndale House Publishers, Inc., Carol Stream, Illinois 60188. All rights reserved.

Library of Congress Control Number: 2024919018
ISBN: 979-8-88928-043-9

Cover Design & Interior Layout: Innovo Publishing, LLC

Printed in the United States of America
U.S. Printing History
First Edition: 2024

Has God called you to create a Christ-centered or wholesome book, eBook, audiobook, music album, screenplay, or online course? Visit Innovo's educational center (cpportal.com) to learn how to accomplish your calling with excellence.

Without Kate by my side for all these decades, I would not have been able to do any of these things—even write this book.

CONTENTS

Glossary xi
Introduction 13

1: WHERE IS HE SENDING ME? 15
2: IN THE BEGINNING 23
3: GETTING AWAY FROM IT ALL (1975) 27
4: THE PEOPLE 29
5: BOTSWANA: TURNING AROUND, FINALLY AND FIRSTLY (1975–1977) 37
6: NEW DIRECTIONS 49
7: TANZANIA (1983–1985) 55
8: WEST AFRICA (1988–1992) 63
9: MENTORS—OR BETTER PUT, MY CLOUD OF WITNESSES 81
10: NEW FRONTIERS: SUDAN (1993) 85
11: SIDE TRIP 89
12: DENTISTS AND ARABIAN NIGHTS 93
13: MOVING ON 99
14: TAKING A BREATHER 117
15: THE BEJA 119
16: THE KIDS' SCHOOLING 123
17: JORDAN: PHASE II (1996) 127
18: STATESIDE 129
19: GOD'S SOVEREIGNTY (1998) 133

20: RAMADAN	137
21: CAMELS, CAMPING, AND CULTURE	139
22: PROJECTS AND PROGRAMS	143
23: MOVING SOUTH (2001)	147
24: PRAYER AS PRIORITY	151
25: GOD'S INTERVENTION	155
26: THE LONG MARCH	159
27: STARTING OUT IN THE SOUTH	163
28: MEDICAL ASSISTANCE	165
29: CATTLE CAMPS	167
30: OUTREACH	171
31: WARRIORS THROUGH AND THROUGH	173
32: KINGDOM HEARTS	175
33: BACK TO THE MIDDLE EAST (2010)	185
34: OMARI	191
35: DRIVING	195
36: STARTING OUT . . . AGAIN	199
37: BLOG POSTS	203
38: THREE MEN	219
39: CLOSING OUT	225
40: PERSEVERANCE AND GRATEFULNESS	229

GLOSSARY

Abaya	a simple, robe-like garment, worn over clothes by Arab women
AIM Air	African Inland Mission
Dishdasha	a long white robe worn by men in the Middle East
Elephantiasis	A painful and profoundly disfiguring disease, often causing severe swelling of the limbs
Karkadeh	Hibiscus tea, drunk either hot or cold
Keffiyeh	Traditional headscarf worn by men in parts of the Middle East
Khwaja	Foreigner
Kjoppies	Rock outcroppings in Africa
Lorry	Large, heavy vehicle for transporting goods
MAF	Missionary Aviation Fellowship
Majlis	a large sitting room for Arab men to gather in
Maktub	Office
Mansef	A traditional Levantine dish made of lamb cooked in a sauce of fermented dried yogurt and served with rice or bulgur
Mantika	Neighborhood
Matatu/Podo Poda	Minivans transporting people in cities on established routes
Medevaced	Airlifted out for medical care

GLOSSARY

Mokoro	Dugout canoe
Moringa tree	A fast-growing tree with multiple uses; also called the "miracle tree"
Palava	Heated argument, often loud and confusing
Punting	Boating in a long boat with a flat bottom, using a pole to move
Rondaval	Circular mud hut
Shamba	Farm
SPLA	Sudan Peoples Liberation Army
Tarmac	Paved roads
Tukel	Mud hut with thatched roof

INTRODUCTION

When I first set out to write this book, I did it for the express reason of having something for my children to remember my wife and me by, once we relocated to heaven. I knew there would be several stories that they either did not remember or actually never experienced. The further I got into writing it, I realized that there was an alternate reason that superseded my original intentions. The kids will still hopefully enjoy it, but there is a much bigger picture to be painted.

My overseas career started in Botswana with the Peace Corps. Kate and my careers together began in Tanzania, followed by Sierra Leone, Jordan, Northern Sudan, Jordan (again), Northern Sudan (again), Southern Sudan, Jordan (again), Amari,* and finally Capestan.*

Spending the last decade or so of our overseas career, which in total is now longer in time than what we have lived in America, mentoring young men who have very few "mature" coworkers still around, I have begun to understand that some of what I have put down in writing just might be of value to the newer generations. I am constantly being asked questions like, *What would you do if this happened to you?* or, *How would you respond to this security situation in the spur of the moment?* or, *What should I do now that I have this information presented to me?* or, *What are the issues I should be looking at in making this decision?* or, *How do you begin discipling someone? Where do you start?*

Hopefully some of the stories that God has allowed us to experience over the past four decades will help to answer a few of those questions. This book is **not** about me, my wife, or my children. It **is** about the faith journey that the

INTRODUCTION

Master has taken us on over these years and how His grace, provision, faithfulness, and blessings have been central to all that we have seen and done.

We have been privileged to work with some of the poorest of the poor and some of the richest of the rich on this planet. Working for years with people who had incredible humility and hospitality, and then later on, for a decade, with people who were filled with arrogant entitlement, was a very challenging walk in our lives. Each of these segments of humanity needs the love and relationship of the Creator who put them on this earth, yet at the same time they will be looking at the words in the Bible quite differently. That made our service, and those whom we worked alongside, frustrating and confusing at times, joyful and exciting at others. Stories from scripture that were effective in one culture were not always very powerful in another. It was a constant learning curve for us.

As we are now in the twilight years of this season of life, we are experiencing an interesting transition. While we don't expect our overseas living and working to be completely finished, it will certainly be reduced—age is stepping into that equation. The journeys will be shorter, but hopefully the spiritual impact will be Kingdom enhancing. We are eagerly looking forward to this next season of life and all that it will hold, yet at the same time we are not going to be rushing it along. We want to continue to be enriched by all that the Master has planned for us as His servants and to faithfully serve Him wherever He has chosen. As Psalm 138:8 says, "The Lord will work out *his* plans for my life." That's good because I would probably mess up any of the ones I made.

Chapter 1

WHERE IS HE SENDING ME?

Miles and miles of green bush. Actually, hours and hours.

"I haven't seen any landing strips down there," I casually commented. The pilot assured me that one would be coming up soon. What I did see over the past few hours were several plane wreckages left to rust and serve secondary usages for any nearby villages.

Ever since living in the north of Sudan the previous years, I had wanted to go to the south. Tried to go several times, in fact. Unfortunately, wars make strange boundaries. And when there are one million square miles that you are dealing with, that leaves a lot of bordering to be dealt with. I had heard many stories and read several books about it, and I had this burning desire to go and work there. Ancient tribes, no permanent roads, diseases unknown in other parts of the world, and almost-constant hunger and famine over the past several decades. And most of the tribes there, I was told, did not know who Jesus really was. After living down there for a few years, I got my hands on a book written by a missionary who lived in Sudan and Ethiopia for fifty years. Don McClure arrived there somewhere around 1927 or so and was ultimately killed by Ethiopian tribesmen in 1977. By the time I finished that book, I realized how "soft" I really was. And this is *after* I had lived in a tent for five years while getting started, finally built a house that my wife would come and live long term in, ran a bush clinic for some years, had terrible bouts of malaria that haven't done my long-term health any good, and started training up a good core of young church leaders.

Flying into Southern Sudan in the early days of this century, while the country's latest civil war was raging, always brought a certain amount of risk. There were plenty of Ukrainian bush pilot cowboys who were constantly dropping off relief supplies or guns or ammo or whatever. They didn't always fly by the normal flight rules and patterns. Quickest way in, quickest way out. We had an encounter with one of them on a flight back from Malakal one day. The pilots we flew with were always very meticulous with their routes, elevations, and destinations, as were most other pilots. This day, we were at elevation, heading south, when out of the blue, coming across our nose at ten o'clock was one of the Ukrainians. I can tell you that when you can see the whites of another pilot's eyes—that's way too close. Because it happened so fast, I didn't have time to freak out, and thankfully my pilot had been flying down there for many years, and this was not the first time he had encountered such craziness. He very quickly took evasive action and uttered a few Christian swear words, while I sat there in the right seat, bug-eyed and trying to swallow my heart back into place for the remaining three hours of the flight.

During the war we always flew up around twelve thousand feet, and when we got close to our destination, the pilot would begin the downward spiral to the landing strip.

Most of these were little brown pencil strips distinguished by the lack of any vegetation for somewhere between seven hundred fifty and eighteen hundred feet. The first time I flew onto the one on the side of a mountain, I remember I kept asking the pilot where we were going to land because I certainly did not see anything that resembled a clearing. I had realized that these particular aircraft were mostly STOL (short takeoff and landing) planes, but that did little for me sitting in the front seat.

"Oh, it's right down there," he replied, with a confidence that was certainly overestimated in my own mind.

I was scanning the ground like a laser beam, looking to see what he calmly stated was indeed there. It was not until our wheels were fifty feet above touchdown that I actually deciphered the walking path that we were about to claim as a landing strip. Maybe six hundred feet in length. Needless to say, as I am now writing this story, we landed, and we took off again successfully. Those pilots are truly amazing in what they can do.

The routes we had to take coming and going from Kenya were most often not "the shortest distance between two points." There were usually obstacles in those pathways, anti-aircraft guns being the one I most recall. Of course, the pilots knew the maximum distance and range of the guns and the routes we had to dogleg to get around them. There was also the occasional fighter jet who might spot us. The good thing with those jets is that we flew so slow, and they had to fly so fast, that they usually didn't bother with us. Plus, the fact that they were going so fast and so high, they probably didn't even see us—most of the time.

So, on that first heart-thumping day that I flew in for a "look-see," I was exhilarated. I really had little idea of what to expect other than some *National Geographic* articles and pictures I had perused as well as a briefing from our team leader, who had visited the area a few times. This was new church-planting work. Starting from scratch in this district. Ground zero. A blank canvas. Just me and the Master—with Him leading the way. I was certainly too green to think any experience I had had up to that point would have me prepared for what I was about to encounter. And I was correct.

"There it is," came the words of the pilot through the headset.

"Uh, where?" was the best I could utter as I looked down at the same bush land that we had been flying over for the past few hours.

"Right there," he said as he pointed out the thin strip of dried brown soil that started my mind racing with stories that I had read about some of the South American missionary pilots landing in very remote tribal areas. Jim Elliot's story was in the forefront. Landing, greeting, killing. As we rolled to a stop, and the plane was suddenly surrounded by a sea of ink-black skin, many of them carrying AK-47s, spears, and other weaponry, that story really came to life. The good thing is that most of them were smiling. That was a good sign. The sign that wasn't so good was the pilot telling me that once we landed, I had to jump out and grab the gear and supplies I was bringing in, and he was headed out. One time, some years later, I even had a pilot ask me to get out at the end of the dirt runway so he wouldn't have to deal with the hordes of people who would surround his plane. I did, and he took off immediately as I scrambled out of his backdraft.

Still, my first sight of every young man thirteen years old and older carrying a weapon was a bit unnerving. These boys were barely into puberty. I realized I was flying into the middle of a civil war zone, but seeing young boys with AKs strapped to their bicycle handlebars or on the crossbar between their legs—that was a bit out of the norm. I had lived in other countries where there was civil war before. Seeing guns was not anything new. Roadblocks with young boys, who should have been in secondary school studying mathematics, shoving automatic weapons in your face was fairly common, though always unsettling. That day, however, those huge white teeth beaming through the smiles on their faces was a most comforting feeling.

"OK, see you when you're ready to come out."

True to his word, the pilot was only on the ground for about five to ten minutes, mostly checking his plane over before the return flight. Watching him leave that first time gave me a sense of reality right then and there. There were no other "scheduled" flights coming in tomorrow, or next week, or, well, not until I scheduled one to come and take me out. It was, in every sense of the word, survival time.

I was met by Wycliffe, the male Kenyan nurse that our company had running the medical clinic for us. We had taken over the clinic from Samaritan's Purse about a year earlier. He had been there this whole time and was easily identified as he was about fourteen shades lighter than the Dinka people. Some years before, Kate and I had learned about African skin colors one evening while at a Bible study when we were living in Khartoum. To us Westerners, there is basically brown skin and black skin. That evening we were schooled by the group we were with, which included Ethiopians, southern Sudanese, northern Sudanese, Europeans, Australians, and a few other nationalities. I honestly don't even remember how the topic of skin color came up, but it was a very illuminating moment in our lives. We learned that Africans have a variety of colors they identify themselves and others by—everything from blue (the very black Dinka would be in this group) to brown (certain Kenyans would fit in here) to yellow (Ethiopians) to pink (many northern Westerners fit in this category). It was quite fun as the Africans went around our large circle and identified where each of us fit in. There were at least a dozen different colors tagged to us. And here we thought everything was black and white.

Wycliffe quickly gathered the things I had brought with me (you never flew in on a plane that was not absolutely full to the maximum weight limit with needed supplies), and we headed to the tented compound that would become my home away from home for the next five years. It was about two kilometers from the clinic and landing strip. It had a kitchen (both inside and outside), a dining hut, two storage buildings, and one mud block room for Wycliffe. They had set up a few safari tents for people like me who came in on occasion. One of them became mine over the next five years. The kitchen, dining *tukel* (round mud hut), and storage rooms were mud-walled and thatched-roof structures, which were amazingly cool in the heat of each day. We screened the windows and door on the dining tukel to limit the number of critters that could enter our sacred area, as we not only ate in there but spent time together playing games and just talking. Some years later we built a fired-brick, three-roomed dwelling for a young couple who came to work with us. The compound was surrounded by a bamboo fence that needed replacing every few years, along with a pit latrine (where bats liked to dwell) and an outdoor shower we fashioned out of a black water storage tank. That was the favorite hangout of the bees because the water was always dripping out of the spigot. Taking showers was sometimes tricky if you wanted one during daylight hours.

Of course, the nighttime brought along all sorts of other various and sundry creatures to deal with—scorpions, snakes (lots, and mostly all poisonous), biting centipedes, mosquitoes (carriers of the malaria that I suffered through several times), hyenas, and an occasional leopard, though I never saw one myself. The local villagers swore to me on a weekly basis that there were lions prowling around as well, but having never seen any evidence of one, I took that as a memory from their grandparents that was passed down in the folklore of the Dinka. Things like black mambas and spitting cobras were much easier to verify, as we killed dozens during our years there. Snake bites were one of the more common reasons for people coming to our medical clinic. Anti-venom was something we always kept around.

On that first trip in, Wycliffe and I took a trip to visit our nearest Western neighbors, about three and a half hard hours to the west in a different district, working with a different tribe. They were living much the same as we were and were engaged with running an oral Bible school as well as other community development programs. More than once during subsequent trips over there we would end up stuck in a mud quagmire or in a flash river or have any number of flat tires, broken axles, or other mechanical maladies. With the nearest AAA about eight thousand miles away, having some basic vehicle repair skills was essential. I once got a radio call from two young ladies, short-term volunteers out to help for a few weeks, that they were broken down on the road, and "would we come and help them out?" Where we lived, deep in the bush, when a distress call like that came in, you always did what you could to assist. Three hours later, and a ten-minute walk from their compound, we arrived to find there was nothing we could do for the burned-out brake linings. Nothing to do but take the girls to their compound, then turn around and make the trip back to Akot in the dark—though not as happy Samaritans! The next day we sent our mechanic to repair the vehicle.

Radio contact was extremely important during those days. We had a base unit on our compound that we used to check in with our office in Nairobi every morning and evening. It was also our contact with the vehicles we had, each of which had a mobile unit, as we traversed the countryside carrying out our work. Because the civil war was still raging at that time, it was mandatory to maintain contact with each other any time we traveled. And not only with those on our team, but with each of the few other organizations that were working in our region. There was a constant exchange of information going on over the airways—where "no go" zones were, where clashes may have broken out, where people may have needed to be medevaced to a hospital, or where someone was broken down on a road.

Speaking of roads . . . that is a relative term. The nearly ten years we lived in Southern Sudan, there were no tarmac (paved) roads in the whole country. Literally, in the last few months that we were there, they were building the very first one from Juba to Uganda. By *road* we mean any possible path between one place and another. I can't recall the number of times that I was driving somewhere and stopped because there was no visible road to follow, when a Dinka colleague would say, "Just keep going straight" or "Turn here." My bewildered looks and subsequent questions probably brought them great humor, or perhaps they just thought, *Dumb White man can't see the obvious road ahead.* But, of course, they never expressed that to me.

Chapter 2

IN THE BEGINNING . . .

My personal journey to overseas service actually started when I was very young. I grew up in a very missions-minded church in Michigan. Every year they would have a two-week missions conference where there were numerous missionaries from around the world attending. Till this day, I can still remember each year eagerly anticipating those two weeks where, when I stepped into the large hall where everyone had their tables and displays set up, I was transported into a world of wonder, and I could use my yet-to-be skill sets in Kingdom service. For reasons unknown, I habitually gravitated to the African section of displays. I could walk right by the China, Japan, Russia, and other country displays with only cursory glances. It was always Africa that had me enthralled. Even now I can recall the names of Ellen Grough, Nancy Perry, the Brandles, and others who served there sixty-plus years ago. Every three or four years, Danny Brandle, a young boy my age, would come stateside, and he would tell me stories of what it was like living in Chad. I was totally captivated. Having missionaries over to our home for meals was also another taste of the life I was sure I would be living. The eventual course to my service there was certainly not straightforward, though.

It was in a fifth-grade Sunday school class at Highland Park Baptist when I first took that step of faith to begin a relationship with Jesus. I wish I could say that it was smooth sailing from there, but the road ahead had plenty of potholes, speed bumps, switchbacks, and deserts to travel over and through. I'm forever grateful for the excellent teaching I got each week in those Sunday school classes. Through the years, it has been interesting to see how verses and songs and stories that I learned in those early spiritually formative years have so very often come back to my mind in times of spiritual drought or even in times of rapturous joy. One example from today—a half century later—is while I'm swimming daily laps in my local pool, I very often sing hymns that I learned before I was fifteen years old. Songs like "Blessed Assurance," "How Great Thou Art," "Holy, Holy, Holy," or "Great is Thy Faithfulness." Even though my brain has learned, and I have sung hundreds of new songs since that time, it is often the ones I learned early on that come to the forefront of my brain.

Growing up in the sixties was an exciting time. Music (still the best era of all time), social changes, Vietnam, drugs, and other tumultuous changes were constantly churning America. I certainly didn't live in a bubble and was riding with the tide and going with the flow. The long hair, which was my first major battle with my father, a bit of rebelliousness, drinking and smoking, and unhealthy choices were all small signs of my pushback to my parents' generation. In some ways I have looked back over that time, where I saw and experienced some terrible things—like seeing friends die from drug overdoses, others winding up in prison, days on end being frittered away—as a waste of several years of my life. At the same time, God has often reminded me of the

IN THE BEGINNING...

2 Corinthians passage, where He allows us to experience suffering and hard times so that we can help others when they encounter similar circumstances. As I moved into youth work on my road back to renewing and growing my relationship with Him, those wandering days allowed me many inroads to talk with youth who were struggling with some of the same issues I had experienced. It's a lot easier to relate when you can say to someone, "I understand. I've been there."

There was about a five-year period where I sometimes look back and think, *What if? What if I had gone straight to college and not gone to trade school? What if I had not moved to Florida but stayed in Michigan?* Even as I began my young adult journey without a close walk with God, I was never at any point deluded that He didn't still have a hold on me, that I wasn't His child, and that He had a plan for my life. I clearly remember the day when I made the decision that I didn't need church in my life anymore. And just as clearly I remember the first day I stepped back into a church on a lonely stretch of road in Tanga, Tanzania, on my way to the Kenyan coast. It had been a long overland journey, hitchhiking from Botswana where I had just completed my time in the Peace Corps.

Chapter 3

GETTING AWAY FROM IT ALL (1975)

That returning to God journey started out in Francistown, Botswana, where I had just spent the past two-plus years as the building control officer, working for the town council. It was the place where God deeply reentered my life. Not because he didn't want to earlier, but simply because he allowed me to walk in my own paths. *Prone to wander, Lord, I feel it. Prone to leave the God I love.* That particular season of life started when I woke up one morning in my rented home in south Florida and had a good, hard look at my life and where it was headed. The result of that reflection was not a good forecast. I confessed to God that I was making a pretty good mess out of the life He had given me, and I needed to get away from all that currently surrounded me. Then and there I contacted the Peace Corps and filled out their application, and six months later I found myself in Gaborone, Botswana.

At that time there were some options as to where I might go, one of which was Tonga in the South Pacific. But due to the seed the Lord had planted those many years before in that church hall, I chose to go to Africa. It's what excited me for so many countless hours, scanning the tables and talking with the people who had planted their lives on that continent. My wife lovingly brings that up often when reflecting back on many challenging years in Africa and the Middle East. "We could be living on some beautiful island where you could be scuba diving every day!" In hindsight, perhaps she is right, but that seed that was so deeply rooted at a very early age just wanted a chance to burst out of the ground and grow, and there was only one way for that to happen. And I've never regretted it. From that first week, while living with a Motswana family and seeing my first twenty-five-foot python slowly slithering down the road, to the day we left Southern Sudan, with all of its scorpions, spiders, and snakes, forty-some years later, it has been one long and exhilarating adventure.

Chapter 4

THE PEOPLE

Above all, our time on the field has been about the people we have encountered. My first close friend in Botswana was Kiatsaba Nsiiwa, who worked in our town planning office in Francistown. Part of my assignment was to train him to take over my position as building control officer after I left. Kiatsaba was older than I was, married and had young children, and was vivaciously full of life. He loved learning and trying new things, like designing and drawing new buildings. He was very helpful to me as I learned how to function in the local culture. It seems that in each and every place I have lived, God has given me someone to guide me along through the inevitable bumps and bruises of language acquisition and cultural learning. The older I've gotten the more I've recognized the importance of this stage of moving into a new land and working with a different tribe or a different clan or a different people group.

In my second tour in Africa, Kate and I lived deep in the bush lands of Tanzania, five kilometers north of Lake

Malawi, whose proper local name is Lake Nyasa. It was about an hour outside of the nearest small town, Kyela. There was a kind of bend in the road at Ipande where we turned right that was about thirty minutes away in the dry season and much longer during the seasonal rains, if it was passable at all. We spent two years there, working on a *shamba* (farm) alongside Doug and Evelyn Knapp. My first day there I met Talian Banda, the manager of the farm at that time, and from that day until we returned stateside, I don't think we left each other's side for much longer than the time we slept at night. To this day we remain close friends and share many of our life's experiences with each other. We have each seen kids born, grow up, and go to school; parents and grandparents pass away and take up residence in heaven; our own selves go back to school and change jobs, positions, and countries; and enjoyed reminding each other of how gracious our God is to us.

Third time around it was Abu Fornah in Sierra Leone. I met him within the first week or so after moving there, and we shared life together for the next four years. As he was a relatively new believer, I had the privilege to mentor and disciple him and watch him grow into one of the local church leaders in our community. He, in turn, taught me the ins and outs of the culture. We went through a lot together as young men, as it was a fairly turbulent time in their history. The civil war that broke out during our third year was horrific (Liberia was the year before). The phrase, *Do you want short sleeves or long sleeves?* was one of the war cries of the time. The translation was, "Do you want your arm or your hand cut off with the machete?" As bad as that became, and it got progressively worse over the years after we left, we were blessed with a time of church growth, both in number and in maturity. Abu was with us from the beginning when we planted a small fellowship in Goderich, about five kilometers from our home, on a dirt road that led down the coast. What

THE PEOPLE

my wife and I didn't know until some years later was that the land with the thatched roof structure that we initially used was formerly a place for devil-worshiping sacrifices!

My next cultural mentor was Ahmed from Iraq. It was during our Arabic-language-learning years in Jordan. Ahmed was a refugee from the first Gulf War, and we spent almost every single day, after my regimented school classes, walking the streets of Amman. Ahmed didn't know a word of English, and I knew precious few in Arabic when we first met. I was introduced to him by a friend who had used him as a language helper the previous year and was now leaving the country. And though I knew I was not going to be speaking his exact dialect, what I did have was a young man who had no other means of support and nothing to do all day long (he was not allowed to work in Jordan). He was an amazing gift from God. Every day a different coffee house or tea house, every day new vocabulary to practice and learn, and very often opportunities to share my faith with him, as much as that was possible with my limited vocabulary. I was not the first one to share stories about Jesus with him, but he certainly got a good reinforcement for the ones he had heard from my friend. Our friendship grew as my Arabic grew. By the end of that first year, he was able to tell me his incredible, two-hour-long story about the first Gulf war and how he and his family got him out of Iraq, the Iraqi army, and into Jordan. In the end, both of us departed the country within a month or two of each other. We were blessed to be able to help him get relocated to an Eastern European country, while our family headed for the deserts of Sudan.

Our first few years in Sudan, my cultural mentor was from the Beja tribe. Frank* was a former Muslim who found the love of Christ too overwhelming to ignore and became an avid follower. We hung around quite a bit—he actually worked for our NGO (non-governmental organization) for some time—and he was instrumental in planting the first gathering of Beja believers in Sudan. He was a wisp of a young man when I first met him, and the many times that he was taken in by the government for sharing his faith left him even wispier. Many beatings, a lack of food, and dreadful prison conditions certainly didn't do his health any good. There is a lot more about Frank later on.

Our second time back in Khartoum I hooked up with Sami.* We were going to be working together for the near future, and he was about my age or maybe a bit older. Sami had some big dreams for sports development, and I was the guy who was going to help him set those dreams in motion. At least that was his mindset. I spent about four years with Sami, and while he was not as close as some of my other mentors, he certainly helped greatly with understanding the northern Sudanese worldview.

When Kate and I moved on to a new assignment, I lost touch with Sami, but I am confident if I went back to Khartoum, I could find him quickly. One thing I remember about him was the day President Clinton sent in missiles that destroyed the pharmaceutical plant there. Highly animated, he exclaimed to me the next morning how, as he was sitting up on his rooftop, the missiles had raced down his street above his house before slamming into the factory. He thought it was pretty cool, though he was sad for the factory owner. He actually asked me why they didn't hit the statehouse instead. An interesting sideline to that story is that a colleague who was in-country and staying with us for a few days had a meeting scheduled with the owners of that factory the very next day after it was demolished! The meeting didn't happen. In fact, he declared himself non-essential personnel and took the next flight out of the country.

My Kenyan cultural guru was Wiki (not the same Wycliffe that was our nurse in Southern Sudan). When Kate and I moved to Nairobi to work in Southern Sudan, we needed some help around the house, as I would be traveling

THE PEOPLE

a good bit of the time. We were attending a local Baptist church at the time, and the associate pastor there was also the one in charge of their fledgling missions program. It was to Simon that I went to ask if he knew anyone whom he would recommend to work as a guard, as well as in our garden. Wiki was that man. This is a friendship that has endured until this day. I have so many stories about Wiki that I will probably have to write a short chapter about him. Close friend, counselor, cultural mentor, language helper, co-laborer in Christ—all of these and more over the years of our relationship.

When I first arrived in Southern Sudan, I met several kind and encouraging young men—Ezekiel, John Deng, Mathiang, and others—who helped me in those initial days and weeks of adjustment. Over the ensuing months, three young servants, Abraham, Isaac, and . . . Gordon, rose to the top to become my inner core of faithful men who guided me, encouraged me, and prayed alongside me. Like some of the others mentioned above, I still maintain regular contact with these men and am encouraged by their steadfastness to the high calling of serving the King. Like many of us, they too have had their share of spiritual and physical challenges. There have been times of failing, struggle, hardship, and sorrow, yet each of these men still serve the One who saved their eternal souls.

Finally, there was actually a group of young men from the Arabian Gulf region who were incredibly helpful in our adjusting to that region. Each of them was a millennial who, along with their families, became some of our closest friends. Without their insights into the local and national culture, we would have floundered much longer during our early years in the country.

Over and over we have witnessed people in foreign cultures who are there for personal interest: the NGOs, the educational tourist, the businessmen looking for the fast buck, or the contract worker residing for a year or two to make a lot of money and live comfortably as an expatriate. For the most part, they have little interest in the cultures they have come to reside in. There are people who come for a two-year assignment, move into a housing compound with pools, tennis courts, restaurants, and convenience shops, and never leave those cozy confines except to go to work. And at that, they often have a driver come to pick them up at the gate and deposit them back there when work is done for the day. We have often met people who have lived in-country for ten to twelve years who can't speak a sentence of the local language, have never visited any of the historical sites, or can count on one hand the number of local homes they have visited. It's really disheartening when we come across these expatriates, knowing what they are missing out on.

There is another category of worker: the international schoolteachers. They are an essential component for most of the UN workers, missionaries, high-ranking local government workers, or business moguls who want their children to have a high level of education. In many cases that is exactly what they get—a far better education than they would get in their own countries unless they were enrolled in pricey preparatory schools. In the international schools their children get some of the highest level of the arts, a worldview that is much broader than they would achieve living in the USA, Europe, or Asia, sports programs that often travel not only to neighboring cities but to countries outside of their own for competitions, and a collage of friends from around the world that they will remain in contact with over the subsequent years. Our daughter was once traveling with a friend from the States through southeast Asia on her way home from Kazakhstan. The two of them just kind of couch hopped from country to country—not because of some cool app that was out there; rather, simply because our daughter knew people in almost all of the countries. Her friend asked

THE PEOPLE

her about halfway through the trip, "Do you just know people everywhere?" She replied, "Pretty much."

I am intentionally leaving out the East Asian and Chinese worker force, as that is a lengthy and complex subject with much history behind it, yet both are an integral force in the development of the African continent. To get a greater understanding of this important segment, read some of Paul Thoreau's books about Africa, such as *The Last Train to Zona Verde* or *Dark Star Safari,* or even *Deep South*—about the southern USA. You will find them very enlightening and spot-on in their depictions.

Chapter 5

BOTSWANA: TURNING AROUND, FINALLY AND FIRSTLY (1975-1977)

The stopover in Kinshasa was only about an hour, but what I vividly remember those many decades ago was the sea of jet-black faces with brilliant piano-white teeth lined along the outdoor railing on the second-floor balcony, the air as thick as a steamy, used washcloth hung out to dry. This was not the Humphrey Bogart *African Queen* or others that I had already seen numerous times. More like the Clark Gable in *Mogambo*. I could feel the excitement racing through my veins. Only another hour or two and I would be planted in Botswana for the next few years. God had already done the first part of what I had asked Him—I was away from all the negative influence that was not healthy in my life. Now it was time for me to step up. Little did I realize how much I would need to do that.

The first couple of months were pretty intense—language study, living in a village *rondaval* (mud hut) for a few weeks, other new cultural experiences, some pretty extreme heat—and that would only heighten as the months went by during that first year. One of my early, old habits that I re-upped was reading. Ever since I was able to read on my own, I devoured books. I practically lived in libraries up through my teens. Early on I discovered a pretty good public library in Gaborone, and I voraciously read books during the entire time I was in Botswana. Some were by classical writers that I had managed to skip in high school—Dickens, Steinbeck, Dante, among others. Some were Christian authors that I had never heard of or read before—Bunyan, Augustine, C. S. Lewis, and Oswald Chambers were a few that caught my interest. Andrew Murray, William Carey, Adoniram Judson, and other biographies were some of the most interesting reads and I'm sure part of God's preparation for the years ahead of me.

Around the third month, with enough Tswana language under our belts to get us into all kinds of predicaments, my Peace Corps colleagues and I ventured out to our assignments. Mine was in the north of the country. I loved Francistown. It was just right. Lots of history on the railway line between Bulawayo and Mafaking, a small population of about forty thousand, and a close-knit expat community, many of whom were from either Rhodesia (now Zimbabwe) or South Africa. From the get-go I recognized that, as a young twenty something, I was in way over my head. Almost overnight I found myself in a position where decisions I was making with other staff were affecting about forty thousand people. It was somewhat frightening and somewhat exhilarating. I was going to need to grow up pretty darn fast. Yes, I was in a country that, at that time, was considered the second-

BOTSWANA: TURNING AROUND, FINALLY AND FIRSTLY (1975-1977)

poorest country on the planet. And yes, I probably had as much education as many of the officials making decisions then. But my lack of having been in leadership positions was certainly a drawback. I know I made a bunch of poor decisions while there, though thankfully I worked on a town planning team that could help overcome or correct most of them. At the same time, the experience I got was huge. Being around other expats who had even more experience in my field was of great value. One was a Danish architect that I worked closely with, and another was an American urban town planner who worked alongside of us.

While my focus was on developing a local and countrywide standardized building code, I also had other priorities both personal and professional. Kiatsaba Nsiiwa was one of those. I had come to train him and work alongside him for a couple of years so that he would be equipped to take my position when I left. The joy and hunger for learning that he brought with him to the job each day was refreshing. He was always full of questions and a diligent worker. On most days when I left the office, he was still plugging away on one project or another. I would say truthfully that I probably learned as much from Kiatsaba as he did from me. Did it all pay off in the end? Well, when Kate and I were in Tanzania about seven years later, we decided to take a trip to southern Africa, going through Zimbabwe, Botswana, and South Africa. I wanted to show Kate many of the places that had significance in my life during those years. When we reached Francistown, I hardly recognized it, even though it was our office who designed it!

The town government leaders had done everything that we had proposed in the first five-year development plan for the town, and even more after that. That was one of those moments that I have relived over and over since then, as those kinds of successes in Africa are few and far between. The continent itself is littered with incomplete or abandoned aid projects that are a blight not only to people's eyes but to the "we have all the answers" of Westerners. Again, check out Paul Thoreau's books for a much more in-depth description. Dambisa Moyo, a Zambian, has also written an excellent book called *Dead Aid* that addresses this continent-wide issue.

On the personal side of growth, I knew from the beginning of this process that it was God who had set this all up. There was absolutely no question about that. It was time to return to my spiritual roots and start the growing process again. The reading I had started doing was the first step in that process. Plowing through books that were enriching to my soul and formative for my future pathways was crucial and certainly did not stop there. That has been a lifelong journey as I have traversed the different seasons of life. It's been interesting to look back at how my perspectives and interpretations of scripture have evolved as I have applied them in foreign cultures.

The number of times that I have been in a teaching position with one group or another and have had a question posed to me about a particular biblical verse or passage that totally stumped me are numerous. Africans and Middle Easterners simply do not think like we do. Their history and worldview demand that they see scripture from different windows than we do. One example of this is from the oral Bible school we started in Southern Sudan. There was a group of young men in class one day, and I was teaching on the story of Jacob. When it came to the passages where it talks about his deceiving and being deceived, the class lit up with animation—but not for the reasons I was headed toward. They all considered him a hero for cheating Esau out of his birthright and blessing. When I tried to accurately point out what scripture was trying to convey, they backed up their side by telling stories of when they got deceived and how the deceivers were so clever. It was a constant struggle to

BOTSWANA: TURNING AROUND, FINALLY AND FIRSTLY (1975–1977)

help them see sin as God does as opposed to how their own cultures declared.

That was not the first, nor the last, time for teaching moments like that. The way one culture looks at scripture is often not how others look at it. There have recently been several books written on the subject—*Jesus through Middle Eastern Eyes* and *Paul through Mediterranean Eyes*, both by Kenneth Bailey, and *Misreading Scripture with Western Eyes* and *Misreading Scripture with Individualist Eyes* by E. Randolph Richards and Brandon O'Brien are just a few examples. These types of books have been very helpful to me as I reflect on how to best teach scripture in the context that I'm in. It's a continual learning and growing process.

Very early on during my days in Francistown, I met an Irish nun by the name of Aine Timoney. At that point in my life, if anyone had told me that an Irish Catholic nun would have a big impact on my life, I would have told them to put their head on straight. But lo and behold, God had this sweet, kind, and full-of-grace woman teach me all sorts of life lessons from a perspective that I certainly had not gotten in the Christian circles I was surrounded by in America. She was an integral part of God's plan to open my eyes to His placement of worldwide servants who did not come from my conservative denominational background. Aine was a different kind of book for me, one that was alive and teaching me different perspectives about how I'd always interpreted scripture. She certainly did not have the same perspective on many aspects of living out Christ in the world that I had. I will be forever indebted to her for unlocking a segment of my brain and heart that I had not known existed.

Aine ran a community center that primarily taught Motswana women how to sew, though there were many other activities that they were engaged in. One of my fellow Peace Corps volunteers, Jane, worked at the center, which was how I even found out about it. Through my years in that town, I watched Aine demonstrate and live out God's love to those women and their families. There were many long conversations with her about faith and how it could and should be displayed in the world. To my joy and delight, I was able to meet up with her twice in the years after our time in Botswana. First, when she came to visit Kate and me in our first home in Florida, and second, years later in the UK when Kate and I found ourselves in London for a meeting. We had wonderful times together, and to listen to her recalling our days together in Francistown was a rich blessing indeed, both for Kate and me. I recently tried to look her up online but without any success. Never did I realize there could be more than one Aine Timoney in the UK. I found many, but not the special one that impacted me so much as a young man . . . until this past month. I found an old letter in my house that had a link to a place in the UK that she was connected to, and lo and behold, the leader of that center knew her and had her email address. What joy when I got a response from her. That twenty-plus-year gap was opened up again.

I had the opportunity to travel a good bit while in Botswana, and on one of those occasions I went down to South Africa, which at that time was still steeped in apartheid. Though that pot was boiling, on this particular trip I went along as a driver for Aine and Jane, and we stayed in a convent there at the invitation of Aine and her fellow nuns. Yet again my preconceived images of Catholic monastic life were shattered. I didn't even know men were allowed in a convent. I had expected to be walking around in silence, observing the holiness of everyone inside, eating out of a big pot in the kitchen, and sleeping on a cot in a four-by-eight cell of a room. Much to my surprise, while at dinner the first night, I had to have an on-the-spot course in how to use all the silver that was laid out so precisely surrounding my place setting. I thought only royalty and the uber-wealthy ate with all those

BOTSWANA: TURNING AROUND, FINALLY AND FIRSTLY (1975–1977)

utensils. My bed that night was something nicer than I had ever slept in before.

***

From time to time, I had opportunities to get out to see and experience the beauty and specialness of Botswana. Without fail, there was something unique always happening during my travels.

"Be careful, there are a lot of them, and they have young babies with them," was my warning to the man who had his hand on the engine of our way-too-overloaded small boat. I had seen many *National Geographic* magazines and specials about hippos in Africa. I was well aware of the fact that more people die from hippos than lions, leopards, or buffalo. What I had not remembered was how fast they are on land; they can easily outrun a man.

So when the man piloting our boat did not listen and got way too close to the pod (herd) of those enormous mammals, with teeth as big as my forearm, three of them started chasing us.

Kerswish, kerswish! Before we knew it, we were the hunted. The huge heads, with the aforementioned teeth, were bobbing up and down in the river and quickly headed in our direction. One soon gave up, but the other two kept coming . . . and were getting closer. This was probably the very moment my high blood pressure started. Everyone in the boat was by now yelling, me included.

"Get to the bank of the river!" I barked, reasoning I could run faster than a plodding hippo. I figured my chances were better there than in that river. (I later learned how precipitously wrong I was). With our boat overloaded with people—eight people in a craft designed for four—and a motor designed for about two, we were not winning the race to flee the mammalian tanks who were chasing us.

By the wonderful grace of God, after a few very frightful minutes, the mothers deemed that we were no longer a threat to their young babies, and they allowed us to go on our way. We were not more than ten minutes further down the river when we were about to pass a safari lodge that I saw the crunched boat. It was approximately the same size as our small boat, but it was in far worse shape. It was prominently displayed in front of the safari lodge as a warning to all visitors *not* to get too close to the hippos. It was literally snapped in two by the steel-crunching jaws of one of the river behemoths.

I wish I could say I learned my lesson that day, but unfortunately about a year later I found myself again on that same river—in a canoe with a doctor friend. We were simply out for a leisurely trek to enjoy the surrounding wildlife and scenery, when all of a sudden, out of the brown water came another perturbed mother. We had not seen any sign of a nearby pod of hippos, but that didn't mean they weren't there. The panic was instant, as there was no motor on that canoe! I'm quite sure our arms were moving those oars about as fast as any propeller could go, but the very worrisome issue was that the hippo had disappeared underwater. My now up-to-date research told me that they can run very fast on the bottom of rivers, and like any submarine, you don't know where it will come up. Vivid pictures of old *Tarzan* movies where the hippos come up under the river rafts and upend the wailing passengers into their open jaws kept flashing through my mind. This time we hightailed it to a nearby, very high riverbank, reasoning that the hippo would not be able to climb the steep slope. I can tell you we sat on that bank with binocular eyes for a couple of hours before getting back in that canoe and making our way back to camp—with hearts still pounding.

BOTSWANA: TURNING AROUND, FINALLY AND FIRSTLY (1975-1977)

The astounding beauty of Africa is something that many have tried to describe but few have done justice to. From tall mountains like Kilimanjaro and Kenya, to the Rift Valley that cuts a large swath through the continent, to vast plains that are home to more animals than most can count, to beaches that rival any others in the world, it is a breathtaking pleasure on the eyes. One of my most memorable times was spending a week in the Okavango Delta with another Peace Corps colleague, Mark Shevory. Mark worked in another town a few hours from Francistown. One day we decided we needed some time off, and the Delta was just the place to spend it. We didn't do much, if any, planning for the trip. Just hitched a ride up to Maun, found a *mokoro* (dugout canoe) driver/poler, and headed out into the vast swamp that covers two million hectares of the northern part of Botswana. The polers stand up in the rear of the canoe and pole in the same manner as punting.

The Okavango Delta, which is now a UNESCO World Heritage site, is a vast inland river delta in northern Botswana. It's known for its sprawling grassy plains, which flood seasonally, becoming a lush animal habitat. The Moremi Game Reserve occupies the east and central areas of the region. Here, the dugout canoes are used to navigate past hippos, elephants, and crocodiles. On dry land, wildlife can include lions, leopards, giraffes, rhinos, and a host of other species. Chobe National Park to the north is a world-renowned park famous for vast herds of elephants and other animals.

The days and nights we spent poling through the rivers and channels of the Delta can never be erased from my memory. Poling past crocodiles sunbathing (and one almost jumping into our canoe as we approached it, thinking it was lying dead on the riverbank), fish hawks dive-bombing the abundant fish life, the silence so pure you could hear an elephant bellow from miles away, and swimming in and drinking from the crystal-clear waters, has never been matched to this day. The awesomeness of God's creation was in living technicolor and surround sound all at once.

The nights were spent camping on little islands of dry land, where the evenings came alive with all sorts of wildlife sounds as if in a movie. For most of our nights, we enjoyed a full moon and were able to actually watch some of the fauna come to life. One evening our guide poled the canoe until about midnight as we were enjoying the amazing views. I think we just about wore our poor poler out that day. We did tip him well at the end of our journey.

About midway through my time in Botswana, I took all of my vacation time that I had saved up and traveled overland up to Kenya. Part of that journey was the opportunity I had to be one of the first passengers on the Tan-Zam/Tazara Railway that had just been completed by the Chinese. I think I might have been the only person in the rail car that I was traveling in. The Tazara Railway is in East Africa, linking the town of Kapiri Mposhi in Zambia with the port of Dar es Salaam in eastern Tanzania. The single-track railway is 1,860 kilometers (1,160 miles) long and was built to give Zambia a port access. It was spotless and actually ran on time. Since the Chinese still operated it, it functioned the way it was designed to. It continued to operate well until the Chinese and European countries pulled out about a decade later. Today is quite the different story.

At the end of the line was Dar, which would re-enter our lives again some years later. This time it was a quick stopover on my way to the Kenya beaches. Heading up the coast from Dar, the first and last larger-sized town was Tanga, about sixty kilometers (forty miles) from the Kenyan border. It was there where my bus ticket providentially ended late one afternoon. As I scoped out the football-field-sized town looking for where I could lay out my sleeping bag for the night, I came across a small church whose doors were wide

BOTSWANA: TURNING AROUND, FINALLY AND FIRSTLY (1975-1977)

open. It had been years since I had stepped inside a church, yet there was something undeniably drawing me inside the structure. As I took a seat in one of the back-row pews, a divine sense of peace suddenly overcame my soul. Then and there I knew something in my life was going to be different going forward. There was not another person in the building, and sitting there listening to the Spirit talk to me after so many years of wandering really refreshed my soul. I spent that night sleeping on the front stoop of the church!

From that sweet memory to one that was not so pleasant in Botswana. It was about a week or two before the Francistown Club tennis championships were due to start, so I decided I needed to make a trip down to Selebi-Phikwe to see my friend Mark who, along with being a great partner in Okavango Delta adventures, was also one of the best tennis players in the country at that time. He was solely responsible for getting me to the level that I was then, and I knew that I needed some good prep time for the tournament. I had managed to hitch a ride in a vehicle with a couple of South African friends and a Motswana friend who were headed to Jo-burg.

Back then the roads were not paved but rather made of gravel. The country simply didn't have the resources at that time to have a good roads system. Even in Francistown, we only had a kilometer or two of paved road. I was sitting behind the driver in the back seat with my Motswana friend. The brothers were up front in the right-hand drive vehicle. At that time, seatbelts were not a thing. As this was about two years into my time there, I had spent a significant amount of time on those roads and knew the danger of driving too fast, but the driver was from South Africa where they had an amazing roads system—mostly paved. Well, the more nervous I got, the more my senses were heightened, and as we rounded a blind curve in the road, there came a big eighteen-wheeler from the other direction. I gripped the driver's seat with all the strength I could muster and held my vice-like grip as long as I could. The driver panicked and started spinning out of control, and our vehicle flipped over three or four times and landed sideways on the edge of the road.

After the initial shock, I pushed my Motswana friend out of the now missing rear window and crawled out after him. He laid on the side of the road, badly injured but not critical. By the time I was out and in somewhat my right senses, I could see the driver, who was badly in shock, running around screaming for his brother. He was nowhere in sight. By the time I located him about twenty meters up the road from the vehicle, it was obvious that he was dead, as his brain was hanging out of his head. I quickly found the driver and tried to keep him away and calm him down. About this time, other vehicles arrived on the scene and began to assist all of us. We were taken into town where we received medical attention. I was the least injured with only a very sore tailbone and banged up shoulder. When I saw pictures of the vehicle a few days later, looking like a metal pancake, with my rear-side window the only pane of glass left in the vehicle, I recognized that it was by the abundant grace of God that I was still alive. He had more plans for my life.

Chapter 6

NEW DIRECTIONS

When the day came to leave Francistown, it was with a lot of mixed emotions. Not all that sure of what was ahead of me but full of confidence that God was in control. A lot had transpired in my life over the previous two and a half years. God had been pruning and replanting me in His rich soil and tender care. I still made a bunch of life-choice mistakes, but over that time, as my walk with Him got closer, I was able to quickly grasp when sin entered and broke that sweet fellowship that was developing. By this time, I knew I was back on the path that He wanted me on. I also knew that I would be returning to this continent, only the next time would be in full-time service to the King. The one final thing I was pretty sure of was that I wanted a life partner to be by my side the next time.

My trip back to the States got off to quite a start when I managed to arrange my transport out of Francistown sitting in the cab of an eighteen-wheeler with two Zambians. It was the only ride I could find headed north toward Tanzania and Kenya. And what a ride it was. It turns out they were headed to Malawi, which was on the route I wanted to go, so I figured that, slow as it would be, at least it was in the right direction. We left in the afternoon and traveled pretty much nonstop. Somewhere in the middle of the night, in the middle of nowhere on the Nata road, in the middle of Botswana, I feel the lorry pulling to a stop. As I groggily tried to open my eyes and focus, the driver looked at me and said, "It's your turn to drive. You do know how to drive this, don't you?"

"Uh, sure," says a cocky, though scared stiff former Peace Corps volunteer. I had never, ever been behind the wheel of something so big and intimidating. The fact that I was coming out of a dead sleep, that it was about 1 a.m., that I would be driving on gravel roads in the middle of the lightless night, and that I didn't even know how to change gears in that contraption, didn't seem to matter. Oh, and did I mention the wild game animals that didn't recognize the roads as something to stay off of? At one point I wound up getting behind a herd of elephants, which brought us to a crawl. Splish, splash, the fresh elephant dung was flung all sorts of ways as I sloshed through it. The really scary part, and the one that ended my tour of driving, was the herd of cattle, hundreds, that we suddenly came upon while moving at a pretty good clip. In that blink of an eye, several things flashed through my mind: crashing into the back of the cattle, killing some of them, and the ensuing *palava* (argument) that would come from it; jackknifing the lorry due to slamming on the brakes and it locking up; rolling the whole rig off to the side of the road, killing the three of us; or swerving off the road into the unknown bush and who knows what all else—each scenario not a very pleasant thought. Somehow, by the absolute grace of the Almighty, that big rig came to a quick stop right at the last tail of the herd, without any of the above-mentioned scenarios occurring. With my heart clearly somewhere on the backs of those cattle, I politely instructed my cab mates that I was done driving for the trip.

After that first leg of the journey, we crossed into Zambia and headed for Malawi. That took me though the southern part of Zambia with two surly drivers. I don't remember at which point they became drunk, but by nightfall, when they came out of their latest roadside pub, I knew that my segment of the journey with them was over. In God's infinite mercy, He sent along three young Indian men in a Toyota pickup, who were headed back to their home in Malawi. When they stopped to pick me up on the darkest of African nights, in the middle of nowhere, I was abundantly grateful and eagerly jumped into the back of their truck. They actually took me to their home, where they fed me, gave me a place to sleep, and allowed me to shower before continuing on to Tanzania. That encounter with the lorry drivers had great potential to turn very ugly, as prior to my angels from Malawi coming along, there were some very harsh threats to my well-being.

It took me about eight weeks to get back to the States on that trip—a few weeks on the coast of Kenya in my tent, eating freshly caught seafood almost every day, and then several more weeks checking out Southern Europe. Both places were to have a much longer impact on me over the years. (Even as I write this, I'm sitting in a beachside cafe called "Hippy's" on the north coast of Samos, an island in Greece). Returning to Hollywood, Florida, I had already determined that one of my first tasks was to find a good place to worship and center my life around. Again, God's sovereign hand was at work, as the very first church I visited wound up being a home for me. It was a place of spiritual growth, a place that provided the woman I love and cherish, the place where I was baptized, and the place that first sent us out on the mission field.

The pastor of that church was a man who had tremendous influence on me. Though not one of the personal mentors God put into my life, he was very much a man full of spiritual wisdom and a good role model. And it was not only me who he had a great influence on. Out of that same fellowship came a multitude of leaders who can, to this day, be found in churches throughout the US and on the mission fields all around the globe. Bill Billingsley was a man who knew how to lead and build leaders. Sheridan Hills Baptist Church was planting churches before it became a thing. Latinos, Haitians, the Polish, Romanians, and many other nationalities were part of their community church-building programs. The family atmosphere that was nurtured at Sheridan Hills could have been a model for the Mormons. The array of relationships that I entered into and grew with was broad, including lawyers, financial gurus, business executives, tradesmen, medical workers, students, insurance men, airline pilots, and a host of others. Not once did they ever give me the feeling that I didn't belong in their circles. Many of them were teachers of Sunday school classes, who helped progress my own spiritual growth. It was the next big step along God's growth timeline for me. Realizing that God uses the everyday man to accomplish His purposes gave me hope that there was a place for me somewhere across those two big ponds that surround our USA.

Sheridan Hills was also the place where God introduced me to my lifelong partner and amazing wife, Kate. When I first arrived at that church, Kate was away at university, and I didn't know she existed. My first Sunday there, I went to a class for young adults that was led by a woman named Dot. Over the next year or two, I would occasionally sit in the worship service with her, and I don't ever remember her mentioning she had a daughter. It wasn't until three years after I had arrived that Kate suddenly appeared out of nowhere—up on stage, singing in a group. By that point I was working with the youth and was heading up some of their recreational sports programs. The volleyball league was one of those. By that time the blip on the radar was getting bigger, and when I saw her on that opening night where teams were formed, I knew which team I was putting myself on. It was during that season of volleyball when my mind was made up as to who I wanted as my future companion. All I had to do was convince her that Africa was going to be a great place to live.

"So, what do you think about living in Africa for the rest of your life?" was how the question popped out as we were driving down Sheridan Street one day.

"I'm good with that," was her response. That was the deal sealer. I knew God had chosen wisely for me.

Chapter 7

TANZANIA (1983-1985)

Kate and I first went to Tanzania about a year after we got married. We were sitting in church one day when a worker from the Tanzanian bush came and spoke to us about what was going on there. Turns out it was a whole lot. The Holy Spirit was pouring out Himself on the Nyakyusa people group, and multitudes were coming to a saving faith in Christ. In fact, the need for help was growing so fast that this man, Doug Knapp, pleaded for some of us to come out and help him erect some church buildings. After the service, Pastor Billingsley came up to us and said, "Mick, you need to go and build those churches." Well, seeing as I was a builder, we assumed that this was clearly God calling. In fact, Kate and I had been in the process of looking for a place to serve overseas for a few months prior to that. Within a few short months, we were on a plane that landed in Dar Es Salam in the middle of the night.

That was to be our first African adventure together, and it was a doozy. It started off with us peering into the pitch black of an African night coming off the plane, walking down the stairs to the tarmac, and looking everywhere for Doug, who was to meet us. He was nowhere in sight. Fortunately, as we would experience repeatedly over the years, God had someone else there. Vestal, a colleague of Doug's, was there to pick up another couple who was arriving on that same plane. He saw these two young white faces looking totally lost and wiped out from two days on planes, and he came up and inquired if we needed any help. When we mentioned that Doug was supposed to be meeting us that night, he just kind of chuckled and said he would help us get to where we needed to be. A flood of relief came over us.

The next morning there was a knock at the door of Vestal's house, and it was Doug. "What are you doing here already?" he asked us straight away. When we told him that he had all of our flight information with the date of our arrival, he looked at his watch as said, "But today is only the 4th. You're not due in until tonight." Turns out his watch didn't recognize the difference in thirty and thirty-one-day months, and he was a day off. Thank the Lord for Vestal.

We spent the next two days crammed into the front seat of a small Toyota pickup. The vehicle had bucket seats with a piece of foam as a cushion for Kate in the middle. She had to continually move her legs every time Doug needed to change gears. When we finally arrived in Makwale, we could understand what it's like to be a sardine in a can. During that trip Doug gave us an excellent orientation of what was going on and what we could expect when we got there. He and Evelyn were amazing hosts and mentors, and the years that followed were formative and educational for both of us.

Of course, when we arrived in Makwale and were shown the small three-room house that would be our home for the next two years, it left a little bit to be desired. In the morning when Doug took us over to check it out . . . well, let's just say it needed some work. Opening the kitchen side door (the main entrance to the house), we were greeted by a water pipe coming out of the wall and a refrigerator that was circa 1930's and ran on kerosene. Not a cabinet, chair, table, or cupboard in sight. The kitchen walls were painted a flamingo pink. The living room had furniture but no cushions to go over the wood frames. It was painted canary yellow. The bedroom actually had a waterbed and a dresser the same era as the fridge. Its walls were painted deep purple. There was no hot water as the Tanganika boiler had yet to be hooked up. That did eventually get connected, but since plastic PVC piping was used and was run through the ceiling, about a month later they melted from the heat, and we had a "steam shower" in our kitchen and bedroom one evening. We had plenty of candles, as there was no electricity except for the three hours each evening from 7 to 10 p.m. when the generator would run, so that was no problem. Good thing we were not yet in the age of technology in 1983!

At this point Kate and my memories diverge. I clearly remember her putting her head on my shoulders and crying a soft cry, wondering what she had gotten herself into. On my side, being a builder, I was just thinking of all the possibilities that we had to make this into our own place. Starting from almost scratch was not all that bad, though that fridge was certainly going to be a project. And in Kate's defense, she has hung around for thirty-plus years of tromping through African bush and is truly my bush babe. I couldn't think of another woman I'd rather have at my side through all the adventures we've been through. She honestly reminds me of Katharine Hepburn in *The African Queen* movie.

From the get-go, I was paired up with a most amazing young man, about my same age, named Talian Banda. For the next two years, we very seldom left each other's side and had some exciting times growing together in Christ.

In subsequent years, it has been Kate and my joy to watch him and his family grow and serve our Master. God chose an equally amazing woman, Atupele, to be by his side all these years. We have also had the rich blessing of helping some of his children go through high school and university. And he himself was appointed as the interim president of his seminary some years back. Unfortunately, they seldom pay him his salary. Just how he and Atupele survive is beyond me but thankfully not beyond God's provision. To this day, though he is no longer leading the school, he is still faithfully proclaiming his Savior and teaching the Good News in the seminary extension schools around Tanzania.

Our time in Makwale went across the board in terms of learning experiences. From planting a tree farm of Moringa trees, to youth work, to building church buildings, to running the shamba, to hosting evangelism teams, to managing a small clinic, to just about everything you can do in the bush. There was never a dull moment over those years, the second year of which we managed the farm by ourselves, as Doug and Evelyn spent a year in the States. That was a huge growth year for Kate and me. Responsibilities we never dreamed of having were somewhat suddenly thrust upon us, but we were definitely up for the challenge.

The time on the shamba absolutely shaped our philosophy of missions. We were able to see firsthand things that were profitable to Kingdom growth and other things that we believed were hinderances. Interestingly, years later when we began the work in Southern Sudan, we used the very same framework, without really thinking much about it, that Doug did when he began his work with the Nyakyusa. When you see and experience something successful, you tend to want to replicate it. That same framework—the inner core group, the larger core group, and then the church leaders—can be seen in the formation of Jesus's disciples in the four Gospels. Biblical principles are hard to beat.

TANZANIA (1983-1985)

Kate and I got to spend a lot of time with the youth groups that were just beginning to take root in the churches there. With Talian by my side, we were able to be involved with them and watch as they tried to live out the scriptures they were reading every day. Some of those young people rose up in the subsequent years to become church leaders and pastors to lead their generation in following Jesus's teaching. There were others, who we saw great potential in, who got caught up in the first three illustrations of the parable of the soils and either fell away from the faith or produced fruit that was not healthy or mature. Providentially, for many years following our time there, the Nyakyusa were the dominant tribe in the Baptist National Convention and were highly responsible for the growth of the gospel all across Tanzania.

Of course, there were plenty of challenges along the way. Snake bites can be, and often are, deadly in the African bush. Black mambas, cobras, pit vipers, green mambas, and others have venom that, if not treated quickly, will cause almost certain death. Once while living here, we had a group of church leaders from the States come out for an evangelism outreach. We had split up into several teams of two Americans paired with one Tanzanian pastor. One day, as one of the teams was walking along a dirt path, a green mamba fell out of a tree and bit Pastor Ayubu on the leg. It immediately swelled to where it looked like he had elephantiasis. Most everyone was sure he was going to die, especially when he refused to go to the hospital two hours away and get some serum. What followed was a mighty time down on our knees that night and the days that followed as he hung in there and enjoyed the grace of God. How he survived, no one knows for sure, but we all attributed it to the mercy of God without a doubt.

During Doug's two decades in Makwale, he produced some terrific agricultural schemes. He was, after all, a trained agriculturalist. He introduced pineapples to the area and had a large plot of them right as you drove up to their house—a converted cow barn. And delicious, they were. He also started a rice scheme where he brought samples from many different rice growing areas around the world and plotted out demarcated parcels of land where we planted them side by side. The natural Makwale rice outgrew most all of them with only a couple species even coming close to the local crop production. The taste was absolutely a winner for the local rice. It could be eaten without any other food or spice to make it better.

At one point, Doug brought a bull in from a famous herd up north and populated/crossbred the local herds with that breed. He also had goat and rabbit schemes that we helped run, especially the rabbit project, which Kate had a big hand in. They made for a scrumptious meal. Doug had gotten some giant, and I mean *huge*, German Giant rabbits from a farmer about four hours north of us and crossbred them with the local ones he already had. We also planted a grove of Moringa trees in the area, with the nickname "the miracle tree." They are extremely fast growing (two meters per year), and almost every part of the tree has some use—from firewood, to medicine, to food, to shade, and other uses. It is a highly nutritious plant that is rich in vitamins, minerals, and antioxidants. Moringa is the ancient and biblical "tree of life" described in the book of Exodus (15:20-25). Its seeds are still used around the world to purify water, just as Moses did. That was a very successful project.

When our time was coming to a close in Tanzania, Kate and I were both confident that this was our life's calling and that we would be back on the field at some time in the near future. We had hoped it would be in Tanzania, but God had other plans in our faith journey. He had allowed us to witness something that so very few workers are allowed to experience—a powerful movement of the Holy Spirit on a people group that changed them forever. I don't remember the exact number that pledged to follow Jesus, but it was in the thousands. To this day, we have personally not seen that replicated again, as God had much harder work for us to engage in. One thing it did help us to understand was that God works on His own time frame, not ours, and often that journey is a long one that includes many touches from His abounding grace. For twenty-plus years, Doug and Evelyn labored (and there were others before them), and then God allowed them to see this amazing spiritual awakening. Most don't get that experience. And there we were, taking it all in like this is what normally happens when you invest your life into God's purposes. You can read of this amazing time in detail in the book *Thunder in the Valley*, which tells in depth the story of Doug and Evelyn's years of toil in Tanzania.

During our time in Tanzania we had become a part of the country team there. We developed some great relationships with others who were laboring in some very challenging areas, and many of those friendships are still intact today. One of those was with a couple who lived about two hours from us up in the mountains of Tukuyu. Though our life paths diverged after our time in Kyela, we continued to be in contact with them through the years, often running into them at various meetings or gatherings. More than thirty years later, Lynn and Olan came to our daughter's wedding in the tea plantations just outside of Nairobi (where they still lived until very recently), and Lynn was actually our family's "go-between" during the negotiations for our daughter April's acceptance of the marriage. She did an amazing job of relaying my demands for a couple hundred cattle, among other things, for me to approve of the marriage. Oh, how very clever that family was! In the end, they gave Kate and me a painting of a herd of cattle on her wedding day as their compliance to my demands. They got our daughter; we got a painting.

Back in the States, where we camped out for about three years, we went almost straight to West Texas, where I was enrolled in a university to finish my bachelor's degree and tack on a master's degree while I was at it. Then it was off to seminary in Fort Worth before heading back to the field. During these study and prep years in the wilderness known as Texas, God blessed us with our two children. As I mentioned earlier, we thought we were headed back to Tanzania, but God had other challenging assignments on His radar for us. Sierra Leone, in West Africa, was just the first one. And while we enjoyed our time in Sierra Leone and learned a lot about living overseas, relating to nationals, learning another language, facing our first few crisis situations, and other essential life lessons, God had even more paths for us to traverse after that.

Chapter 8

WEST AFRICA (1988-1992)

Our second landing together in Africa was in Freetown, Sierra Leone. It was on a poor corner of West Africa, surrounded by other poor countries. A sector of the continent that had been traditionally harsh on Westerners, and in particular missionaries, and was often referred to as the "White man's graveyard." As a personal confirmation of that, a colleague and his family, who came out with us, were living in a nearby country when his wife contracted malaria. One afternoon she wasn't feeling so well and sat down in her recliner to rest. When he went to bed, she told him that she was just going to stay in the chair for a while longer. When he woke up in the morning, she was still in the chair but not breathing. A very sad and tragic reminder of the perils of working in that environment.

That was not the only time we were to come across tragedy while on that side of the continent. Our years in

Sierra Leone were filled with the challenges of being new to the field, even though we had already been in Tanzania together and I had been in Botswana. This was the first time we felt like we were permanently planted there for the long haul, like an oak tree in the pastures of a farm, with roots going deep and a focus on the far ahead future in all that we planned. And for the first time, we had children with us.

We lived up above a mission guesthouse, which had its blessings and challenges, though the former definitely outweighed the latter. We were always having people pass through, using the facility to catch their breath or as a landing spot for a shopping trip to the capital. It was a way to catch up with up-country folks and all that they were involved in, in the bush. I was rather fortunate in that my job as a building coordinator for the convention allowed me to do a good bit of traveling around the country. Most of that time, Kate stayed behind with the kids. We had purchased a second (personal) vehicle so she could be mobile when I was on those trips. Whenever I could, which was most of the time, I would make day trips so as to be home at night to be with Kate and the kids. That made for some very long days, as the nearest project we were working on was two and a half hours away. Some were four hours or more. On those days I would leave very early in the morning so I could make it back before it got dark. Even in our early days, there were always roadblocks, some by the military, some by rabble-rousing, machete-wielding, gun-toting youth, so it was difficult to really put exact time frames on travel. Some roadblocks were simply checkpoints, but others were thugs trying to get bribes or any other valuable goods to line their pockets. That time was good preparation for the years ahead. Roadblocks in Africa are almost like traffic signals in the West—they are everywhere.

The urban variation of a roadblock are the traffic police. Pretty much the same in each country, with a few exceptions.

Some, like in Sierra Leone, were open and matter-of-fact about the bribes. As very few drivers actually had licenses or a perfectly running vehicle, there was always a ticket-able offense that could be charged. The minibus and *matatu* (poda poda, minivan) vehicles were particular targets. Holding up a group of twenty people all in a rush to get to or from work was an easy mark. But rather than go through all the hassle of lost time or income, it was just easier to hold your money out the window as you passed by the officers standing in the road. If you decided to skirt past the police, you were taking a risk that they had seen you, and your next time through you were sure to be stopped and given a hard time—and a steeper "fine." Over the years we heard all manner of excuses, pleading on behalf of this system, but they never did hold much water. Paying the police a salary that is enough to put food on the table each day is one quick solution. Corruption is corruption, and when a poorly paid civil servant is watching his president and top officials packing away millions and billions in overseas banks and property by unscrupulous means, he too will be looking for his opportunity to line the pockets of his family.

One of the additional tasks I had while we were there was teaching in their seminary. The only other professor in the theological education department was Valcarcel, the president of the seminary at that time. Though we did not know it back then, both of us were getting our seminary education at the same school in Texas some years before. That teaching time in Sierra Leone was such a joy for me. Working with the young men who would be going out through the Sierra Leonean bush, teaching the scriptures and spreading the Good News was a huge privilege—and pleasure. It would not be the last time that I found myself in a teaching position in Africa.

It was during our first few months in the country when we had our first family crisis. God used this time as a lesson for us that He was in control of everything, even when things looked impossible. There would be many more instances where that would be revealed over and over again. Caleb was about seven months old and one day produced a life-threatening hernia. We rushed him to the local expatriate doctor in town, and she told us that he needed surgery ASAP but that there was no doctor in Freetown that could do that. We needed to go to neighboring Liberia where there was a mission hospital with some terrific surgeons. There were all kinds of reasons that that would not be possible in a quick manner. Our passports were with Sierra Leonean immigration, and it was closed for the weekend. There was only one flight out to Liberia, and that was the next day. We had no visas to enter Liberia. And on and on. Two panicked parents, new to the country, looking at a strangulated hernia that could explode at any minute on our seven-month-old son. *OK, Lord, Your turn. Show us Your sovereignty.*

Things happened so fast, and with such divine providence, that I hope I record this accurately. When we informed Steve, our business manager, of the situation, he rushed down and called a friend in the immigration office and begged and pleaded for our passports back (how he got in, I honestly don't remember). By now we were throwing emergency supplies into a travel bag (very good training for later in life) and waiting anxiously to hear from him. Some hours later, passports in hand and tickets having been purchased for that flight to Monrovia, we rushed to the ferry to go to the airport. We were literally the very last vehicle on that ferry. Missing it would have meant missing our flight.

Finally, at the airport an hour later, Steve rushed us inside and told us to stand right by the exit door to go to the plane. You see, in those days, there were no reserved seats. They sold however many tickets they wanted to—often more than could fit onto the plane. It was first come, first seated. Once the plane was full, the rest of the ticket holders were out of luck. It was like the Kentucky Derby starting gates. Doors opened and a mad, chaotic rush to the plane about one hundred yards away ensued. Being much younger and in good shape at that time, I made sure my family had seats on that plane!

That was not the end of the affair, though. Once in Liberia where we were met by their immigration officials, we explained our situation and offered to purchase visas then and there, on the spot. Unfortunately we were responded to like refugees trying to sneak into the country. No way could we enter. Depression, anxiety, and fear all rushed to the surface. Then along came Fred, who was the assistant regional leader of our mission, accompanied by a Nigerian doctor who was visiting him, to save the day. He explained our desperate situation and promised to do all the required steps to get the correct documents for us. Still, the official did not want to let us enter . . . until he asked to see the actual hernia on Caleb. When I unfolded his diaper, the official's eyes got as big as watermelons as he looked at a bulging lump the size of a man's fist, and he promptly signaled us to go straight to the hospital. The next morning, Caleb had his successful surgery—by the very same doctor who had set my broken foot when I was twelve years old in Michigan, twenty-five years before. What are those odds?

That was not the last trauma episode for young Caleb. Before he was three, we endured two more heart-stopping incidents and recognized that he had a very special angel watching over him. The first of the two was perhaps the scariest. One day, as we were sitting around talking and finishing lunch around our cable wire table I had made, we all of a sudden heard a commotion coming from our neighbor's yard. The little kids that lived there were screaming at anyone who would listen that Caleb, who was all of eighteen months old, was up on the top of our roof!

That morning, I had been up there repairing and cleaning the water tank, and the ladder, which was about two-plus stories high, was still leaning against the side of the house. How he even got up there, we have no idea, but what got his attention was the scalding heat of the tin roof. Once he got off the ladder (trying to be like Dad?) and onto the roof, he realized that those sheets of zinc were really hot, and he began to cry. The neighbor kids saw and heard him and joined in with their pleas to get him down before he fell. When I realized the gravity of the situation, I literally ran out the back of our second-story house and jumped from the balcony to the ladder—thereby avoiding having to go downstairs and back up the ladder and wasting valuable time—in what I later discerned was not a very smart move on my part. With my heart somewhere in my throat, I reached Caleb before he made any attempt to remove himself from that uncomfortable position.

The second incident occurred on our screened-in rear veranda, where we had our washer and dryer hooked up. We also stored items there that we didn't particularly need around the main part of the house. One of those items was a solid-core, mahogany wooden door that was leaning up against a wall. It had been there since we moved in a couple of years before, and we had hardly given it a second thought all this time. Yet one day, out of the blue, I felt the Holy Spirit whisper to me to go get Caleb off that veranda. No sooner did I pick him up into my arms and begin to walk away than there was a thunderously loud crash behind me that took by breath away. That very door that weighed five times what my son did fell flat to the ground in the very spot that Caleb had been playing. It would have crushed him like a pancake. An undeniable moment of mercy from God that we will never forget.

For reasons unknown, April never did have any of those critical encounters, except possibly one that she and our whole family had along a Kenyan "road." That was a bit later on and a few countries down the road. Unfortunately, however, April has had several close calls with vehicle accidents while living in the States.

During our almost four years in Sierra Leone, we never did have a telephone system. If you wanted to communicate with anyone else, you owned a two-meter radio system. One for your house, one for your vehicle. At all times on the road you were in contact with someone. Around the fourth year of our assignment, they really became crucial. One day, as usual, I took our kids to school in the morning. After dropping them off, I headed to a colleague's house to take care of some business. As we were casually talking away while looking down into town from their hilltop home, there was a sudden and loud burst of gunfire. Though the center of town was probably five kilometers away, the sound was unmistakable. Turns out, that was the beginning of the coup in '92 that erupted the country into their vicious civil war. The eleven-year-long war was estimated to have killed over fifty thousand people. Thousands were maimed and their limbs amputated. Half the population was displaced. Almost all the people of Sierra Leone were affected by the war.[1] Immediately we called the US embassy on our two-meters and asked what was going on.

"We are in a lockdown situation. There is a military coup attempt in town. Go back to your homes now, and keep in touch from there," the American government official's voice screeched.

"We just dropped off our kids at school. What are we supposed to do about them?" I replied.

"Just leave them there and we'll take care of them," the official said.

---

1. Christina Mammone, "The Conversation," Finders University (June 22, 2023).

As I looked incredulously at my radio and thought of the absurdity of that statement, I just signed off, jumped into my double cab Toyota, and raced back to the school. It was only about ten minutes away, but I had to pass by the army barracks—which by then was a flurry of activity surrounded by active fire in all directions—to reach it. Successfully arriving at the school with no bullet holes in my vehicle, I made my way to the headmaster's office only to find that he was out that day (and for the rest of the week with a case of typhoid fever) and that my daughter's teacher was the in-charge that day. As we talked over crucial decisions that needed to be made, I realized that they did not have a functioning radio at the school. Hundreds of kids, one kindergarten teacher in charge, the city in chaos, and this poor woman had no communication line with anyone. My first decision was easy. My kids—and my colleague's child—were coming home with me. The second decision was much harder, though I was never in doubt about what was the right thing to do. I left my two-meter radio with her so she could have a communications line with outside sources, particularly the embassy.

I had never once been without my radio since being in the country. It was like a millennial and their cell phone in today's world, only ours was meant for the main purpose of security. As I pulled out of the driveway to try and make it back to our home, I felt naked. *No communication.* What would I do if we got stopped by the military and taken in? What if one of those stray bullets hit one of us in the vehicle? What if the vehicle broke down or was hijacked (as often happened during those hectic days)? The questions were coming fast and furious, and the answers all led to the same place: God knows what is going on, and He is sovereign. Trust Him. Of course, that didn't stop my heart from racing faster than a NASCAR stock car.

As I made the right turn heading back through the insanity of the military barracks, I firmly instructed the kids to "get down and stay down." Those words went unheeded as all the way back to our house I could see in my rearview mirror little bobbleheads poking up and down. Getting through those barracks was my first relief. Now I needed to pass the president's home, which was up on the backside of the hill where we lived. No luck there. As I had anticipated, the road was already blocked by the military.

It was at this point that I realized that there are often reasons for things happening that we are not aware of in the present time. Some weeks prior to this day, a lady in the Wilberforce church had suddenly died. The local believers said she had a curse put on her. She was about twenty-five—in perfect health one day and dead the next. No autopsies were done back then. Very sad time for our family. It was my vehicle that was used as the hearse for her funeral. It was up on top of the hill overlooking the president's home. When taking her from the church to the burial site, we had to traverse a tiny pathway that the vehicle barely passed over. When I reached that first roadblock, I recalled that pathway and decided it was worth a shot at getting us home. Sure enough, as I crept down that rocky pathway and came to the main road to turn right, there to the left sat the roadblock on the other side of the president's home. Hugh sigh of relief as the only other way to get home was to take a road that went perilously close to the center of town where we did not want to go. And all with no radio contact.

Kate must have been very worried, though I told her what I was going to do prior to surrendering the radio. The parents of the daughter we now had at our house were also quite concerned. Those radios really came in handy as it was about three days before her parents could lift their heads above the ground in their home—which was adjacent to the military barracks—and come to collect her. After they left

Sierra Leone, they moved to another country to work with Central Asians.

For the next five days, we crept around our second-story house on hands and knees as the sound of gunfire was everywhere. Since we lived on a main road, we had a bird's-eye view of much of what was going on outside our walls. Late one afternoon, a truckload of military pulled up to our gate and tried to get into our compound. We had a guard at that time who was quite old but quite wise as well. As the soldiers kept demanding to be let in, while our family was crouched beneath the upstairs windows watching and listening with heaving chests, he steadfastly refused to unlock the gate. He told the soldiers we were away, and we had taken the keys with us. I could only imagine that it was not only that one lonely old guard who kept them from shooting the lock to pieces and coming in to loot our place; rather, like in the book of Kings (2 Kings 6), the Bible describes how God provided an army of angels leading horses and chariots of fire to protect the prophet Elisha and his servant, and He opens the servant's eyes so that he can see the angelic army surrounding them. Maybe our guard didn't have his eyes opened to the army that was behind him, but perhaps those on the outside did see them. At any rate, after a rather testy confrontation, the soldiers moved on to other hunting grounds.

We learned a lot from that stressful period. Unless you have some sort of training, which many companies and organizations now do, you can find yourselves doing the strangest things. I remember Kate asking me on one of those chaotic days, "Why are you counting the empty Coke bottles in the crate?" I can't even remember what my answer was. About the fourth or fifth day of the coup, my son, who was about four at the time, and I went outside and started trimming the bougainvillea bushes that grew up in front and on top of our wall that ran along the road. We lived on one of the main roads in town, and there was no shortage of confiscated vehicles racing past in those hectic days. Why we chose that time to do that, I'll never know, but I do remember a vehicle full of soldiers suddenly coming to a stop in front of our house. There was a definite moment of panic right then, until out of the cab hops my doubles partner in tennis, who was also the reigning singles champion in the country. He was an officer in the army and told me he was just stopping by to make sure we were all safe. To be quite honest, it took me a while just to decipher who he was behind all the weaponry that covered him and his fellow soldiers. He was certainly not in his tennis attire. Again, those lessons learned would come in handy down the road.

About a week into the coup, the US sent in some Special Forces guys to secure the airport and help evacuate the Americans. The airport is located on a peninsula, and you had to take a ferry across the water to reach it—or you could drive a very hard four hours around to it. So, a hotel was secured, an announcement was given over the aforementioned two-meter radios, and we were told that we could take one carry-on size piece of luggage each. We had twenty-four hours to get ready and meet at the rally point—if we decided to go—and that was strongly encouraged by the State Department. From there we would board a hovercraft to the airport.

Our whole team gathered at our home to discuss what we should do as a group. Two of us, myself and another colleague, didn't think we should leave. The others voted to evacuate. It was a majority rules decision that would come back to haunt us when it came time to return. Turns out that only the Americans and the British left. Everyone else stayed. That didn't go over well with our national partners. To be fair, this was only a year after the Liberian disaster, which was fresh on everyone's mind. When that country imploded, a rash of evacuees wound up in our town, and we picked their brains for as much information gathering as we could, so we might be better prepared if things went south in Sierra Leone—which they did.

Once at the airport, there was the visible and respected presence of the US military. National soldiers who were also there took a wide berth when passing them on the tarmac. I'm sure there wasn't more than about three square inches of the American soldiers' bodies that wasn't covered with some sort of weaponry. They were prepared. And one thing that stands out with every member of our family was the food they brought in to feed us while we were waiting to board the C-130. Boxes and boxes of Girl Scout cookies, mixed nuts, sodas of all kinds, and other goodies that none of us had seen in years. Almost made the whole affair worth it. My son can still remember going up into the cockpit of the plane with me to see the pilots who were flying us out. Experiences like that tend to stick in one's mind.

Coming back into the country after a couple of months in limbo in another West African country certainly did not follow anyone's script. A few of us men went in first to assess the situation, particularly the safety aspects. By then most of the craziness of the first several weeks had calmed down. There was still a lot of tension in the country as a whole, with a lot of that coming from a neighboring warlord, but everyday living seemed to be doable. One of the surprises that I found when I walked back into our home was the deep freezer we had sitting just outside our front door in the upstairs hallway smelled like nothing I had ever smelled before. As there had been no electricity for weeks after the coup, I was in for a surprise. Upon opening it, I found thousands of maggots had had a field day with the meat that was in there. How I got through the many, many days of cleaning that up without puking my guts out, I will never know. I certainly did not have any surgical masks to help me through those days! It took weeks for us to get the odor

WEST AFRICA (1988-1992)

out of that freezer after using every single hack known to man to clean and exorcise that stench. Mind you, this was before the internet was around to give some handy tips, but I remember using charcoal, newspapers, bleach, soap, water, and any other thing that was suggested to us. I think it was about two months before it was usable again. It was many years after that before I forgave my sweet wife for leaving that food in there. In her defense, she says she left a note for our house girl at that time to take all the food in there to her home for her family. Unfortunately the note was in a packet with the house girl's salary, and she gave the packet to her husband without ever seeing the note herself. In all fairness, she probably had more pressing matters on her mind, like, *How do I stay alive?*

That was not our only challenge. The national body that we worked in partnership with was not very forgiving of our "fleeing" when things got rocky. Most of the other foreign nationalities stayed behind, kept their heads down, and endured the aftermath of those early days. It was a fracture in the relationship that we never really recovered from. Within the year, everyone on our team had left for other assignments. As our family was due for stateside assignment/furlough, we were only back in-country for three to four months, but once back in the States, we knew we would not be returning. God had another path laid out, and it didn't take long for us to find it.

One of our greatest joys of those early years in Sierra Leone was planting our first church. It was on an old, pot-holed, road, which was better traversed on the dirt to the side of the road, about five kilometers outside of town along the coast. It started out in a thatched roofed structure with mud walls about three feet high. If we were lucky, we could cram about twenty bodies into it, though there were seldom that many in attendance during the first couple of years. What we learned during our last year in-country was that

that site was a former demon-worshipping and sacrificing site. No one wanted to tell us because they were afraid we would never come back there. Hopefully our perseverance and faithfulness during those days and the message that we continued to bring each week showed that community the power that was behind the truth we were exposing them to.

We learned that a lot of blood, sweat, and tears goes into the perseverance it takes to start new Kingdom work in a place that had been controlled by Satan for years upon years. There were many Sunday mornings when we woke up and had to push ourselves to make that five-kilometer journey to what seemed to be a lost cause in that community. Little did we know that during our last year, Goderich Baptist Church would build a new building on other land in that community, and it would become one of the strongest churches in the Baptist Convention. A lot of that success was due to the good leadership of the young pastor, Augustine, who came out of perhaps the best of those more established churches and led those people with wisdom, kindness, and understanding. Sam Sesay did an amazing job of mentoring Augustine, as well as others, and the Baptist church in Sierra Leone has been blessed greatly by his leadership.

The Sunday that the church chose to celebrate their new building is one we will not forget. I think half the community came by just to witness the opening of the new structure. As it was one of the larger buildings in the area, it naturally drew a lot of interest. There was a lot of African pomp and circumstance during the day, and it was one of great joy for everyone. The culminating experience of the day was the meal that was served afterward. By this time, we had lived in the country for about three years and had eaten all manner of interesting new foods—from barracuda steaks to palm tree maggots—but one that we all had great memories of was the "green slime." In essence it was a delicious stew of sweet potato leaves cooked in palm oil and sometimes had fish mixed in. West Africa is renowned for its very hot peppers, which are a prime ingredient of this dish. Caleb, especially, knew of their *fire power*, as when he was still quite young, he got into a large bowl of them after our house girl had set it down outside for them to be cleaned in the water. All of a sudden, we hear this shrieking coming from Caleb. By the time we reached him, his face was already swollen, and his eyes were in great pain. Thankfully our house girl knew to smear him with palm oil to alleviate the suffering. Seeing his face in the two-tone red (peppers) and yellow (palm oil) was quite a sight, but due to the pain he was in, it was not the time to enjoy laughter.

Now it was the rest of our family's turn to taste this heat firsthand. By this point in time, we had all tasted and eaten our fair share of green slime. Each of them had varying degrees of heat registering. Sometimes it was mild-hot, other times flaming-hot. This one had our eyes watering before it even got into our mouths. All I can say is, don't try to eat a bowl of very delicious green slime without having ample water on hand—which we did not. Within the first few minutes we totally guzzled all the water we had with us and were left to carefully measure how much sizzling of our insides we wanted to inflict upon ourselves. Balancing great taste with fiery mouths is a delicate matter.

I remember another very significant day in the life of the Sierra Leonean Baptist churches. We had been there for about three-plus years, working in that community, and a number of people had come to know and follow Jesus's teachings. Many were ready for baptism, so a day was planned for a joint church dunking in the Atlantic Ocean. I had never participated in anything quite like this before (or since), where about sixty to seventy people would be baptized. I would be working alongside Sam Sesay, a local pastor, and together we would be dunking two at a time. That in itself made the day memorable, but there was one other small incident that would highlight it. About the middle point of the line, coming out to me in the water, was a rather large woman. Quite large. As we were in the shallows of the ocean and in a somewhat mucky area, the ground under us was a bit soft in places. Well, when this woman came to me, I silently lifted a prayer to God for extra strength for what was to come. Low and behold, as I dunked her, I took a step back to gird myself and stepped right into one of those soft, mushy holes, sinking down about a foot. I literally had to muster the strength of Samson to bring that lady back up out of the water. She will never know how close I came to bringing her straight to Jesus that day.

There was another valuable lesson that I learned over the subsequent years that was directly related to our Sierra Leone experience: invest in people, not in things. My job assignment was to lead the building department of the convention. I worked alongside Wolfgang Brunssen, an architect from Germany, and a young man named Patrick from Sierra Leone. Wolfgang did most of the office work, and I focused on the field work. It was a sweet relationship where both of our skill sets were used to their maximum. Patrick was our office apprentice, who we were to train to do our roles in the future. There were a lot of challenges that went along with that, yet we managed to help him through some character-building times and to develop into a competent colleague.

During my years there, we built a convention center with housing for about one hundred, schools, houses, churches, and other structures. When we left the country almost four years later, I felt pretty good about leaving behind some buildings that had the potential to better the church as a whole. Within five years, most of those structures were burned down or destroyed in the war. What wasn't destroyed were the people who survived the atrocities. Patrick still had the knowledge we trained him in to build or rebuild what had been destroyed. Sam Sesay, Pastor Augustine, Abu Fornah, Pastor Kamara, and other church leaders still retained all the knowledge and training we had imparted to them to grow and strengthen the church. The women were the most resilient of all and are certainly in the forefront of what is going on today in the convention. This whole experience was something that shaped all of our future work in the years ahead. And yes, there is a time and place to invest in structures and projects that will benefit communities and countries and conventions, but they should certainly not be the focus of our efforts in building the church.

There is a great verse in Matthew 6:20 that says we should "store your treasures in heaven, where moths and rust cannot destroy, and thieves do not break in and steal." Those years in Sierra Leone certainly made these words come alive for us, especially when the civil war broke out and everyone's lives were turned upside down. Though many of our earthly belongings survived those early months of the war, when we returned to the States for some R & R several months later, we packed everything up and stored it in a friend's house. By the time we knew where God was redirecting us, and we requested our stuff be shipped to that new location, many things we had owned either went missing or were eaten by the ravenous termites that called West Africa home. It was a hard lesson to find out that Grandma's chair and our old oak dining table were among the items that succumbed to those pesky insects. Along with those items, my gold-plated hammer that I was given upon graduating trade school also disappeared. Hard but valuable lessons learned about holding on to *treasured* items in this life.

Another part of that lesson-learning experience was our leaving a country embroiled in the early months of a years-long, brutal civil war and heading to the States where we would again be safe. As our family disembarked from the airplane in Ft. Lauderdale into the waiting arms of grandparents, Kate's dad remarked to us, "You guys are lucky to be here now. This airport is about to close down for the storm." We had no idea what he was talking about as this was in the days before mass internet and social media, and news still traveled slowly to other continents. Turns out, we were a day ahead of Hurricane Andrew, one of the worst storms in history, and we had to immediately set about boarding up and preparing our furlough house for the storm.

Since we were in the evacuation zone, we spent the next several days at Kate's parents' house where we listened to the roof creak and groan all through the first night when the hurricane passed over us. The following weeks were spent going down south of Miami each day, helping unravel trees and debris from badly hit neighborhoods, as well as taking and giving out food and water to everyone who was around. The devastation was immense. I remember seeing a ten-inch *I beam* bent and twisted like a straw. Being a general contractor, I knew what power that took to mangle it.

So, just when our family thought we had left one of the worst possible situations we could be in (an African civil war) and were headed for the calm, known, and safety of home sweet home in America, God reminded us that we live and breathe at His pleasure, and we are on this planet to be faithful servants to Him, wherever and whenever He desires. Safety and peace do not depend on location!

Chapter 9

MENTORS—OR BETTER PUT, MY CLOUD OF WITNESSES

In each place that God has taken us to serve Him, He has provided me with a mentor to help me navigate my weaknesses and hone my talents. Having wiser, older men around and being able to ask them questions and get wise feedback was instrumental in my growth as a young man. In Tanzania it was Doug Knapp, with his heart of grace overflowing each day that he served in Makwale. At Sheridan Hills Baptist Church in Hollywood, there were several men who had a valuable influence on my spiritual maturity. Bob Barnes, who is still the CEO of Sheridan House Family Ministries, and Clell Coleman, the former associate pastor, are two that really stand out. Being around and working with both men in their leadership roles was very valuable to me as I also stepped into those types of roles.

In Sierra Leone it was Bert Dyson and Fred Levrets. Both displayed patience and grace in abundance, especially when it was not called for or expected. Bert had spent his first thirty years or so of ministry in Nigeria until one day our leadership came to him and asked him to open up the work in Sierra Leone. He and his wife, Ruth, graciously agreed to come and did a good job of getting things rolling. Little did Kate and I realize what a role model they were for us as we were asked to do the same thing three times later in our career. Bert was a gifted teacher both in schools and with young men. From our first days in the country until we left four years later, Bert poured into me the wisdom of a godly saint who had walked with the Lord with much graciousness over those decades. One of my failures on the field is that I was never able to reproduce the gentle spirit that he, and others, guided me with in those early years. I will forever be grateful to God for allowing Bert to be such a good influence and discipler to me. When I made mistakes, he let me know it, and then he explained to me how I could have done better. Until very recently, Bert sent me notes of encouragement every now and then. He recently relocated to his eternal home in heaven. He had been married to Ruth, who taught Kate numerous lessons about life on the field, for sixty-three years until her passing some years before him.

When Bert and Ruth left the field for medical purposes, Fred Levrets stepped into my life and did a great job picking up where Bert left off. Fred was a very wise man, who also happened to be the associate regional leader at the time. When the war in Liberia broke out, they relocated from Monrovia to Freetown—lucky for us. One of the great things about Fred, though he, too, was incredibly kind, was that he would always stand up for what is right. I clearly recall the time that he stood by my side and had my back when unfounded accusations came my way for conduct that was seen as unacceptable to the national country Baptist leadership. Fred helped me to navigate that situation with delicacy and truth, and in the end, everything turned out well.

MENTORS—OR BETTER PUT, MY CLOUD OF WITNESSES

Eddie P. fit more into the category of a colleague/friend than a mentor, though he was very gifted in working with the multitude of journeymen (two-year term workers, in their early twenties) and other short-term workers we had come our way in Sudan. Watching how Eddie walked alongside these young workers was part of my mentoring, even though he didn't know he was doing that. The two of us had many opportunities to work together on several projects we had going at that time. I owe a lot to Eddie's creativity and vision casting abilities.

Then there is DB, Dwight Bass. Neither of us can accurately remember when our paths first crossed, only that it was quite some time ago. Having both served in East Africa for decades, it is not surprising that we intertwined often. Being roughly the same age, having somewhat similar experiences, and knowing a lot of the same people, makes for a very interesting and cherished friendship. I will say that I probably haven't had another spiritual friend like DB in my whole life. Mixed in with a lot of laughter, all kinds of hyperbolized stories, and some gut-wrenching ones as well, is a deep friendship rooted in the joy of living for the King. There is seldom a conversation had that does not probe the depths of His love for us and how our relationship with Him is growing and being challenged continually.

And finally, there was Donald.* Kate and I had known his parents when we worked in Tanzania years before. They were close friends of the Knapps. Donald was not around at that point; I think he was in university in the States. Years later he and Miriam* were our supervisors when Kate and I opened up the work in Amari. It was Donald's wisdom and his trust in us to follow the leading of the Spirit that allowed the work there to be where it is today. Of course, his wife, Miriam, was an equal influence on many of the decisions that were crucial to the work there. For over a decade we enjoyed an exceptional partnership in working for the Kingdom. Even when we moved from there to our next assignment, they were crucial in the decision-making process and continued being our leaders.

Chapter 10

NEW FRONTIERS: SUDAN (1993)

"Have you ever thought about CSI?" The question was directed to me from a colleague while we were at a stateside conference. Cooperative Services International (CSI) was a new wing of our organization that was focused on using creative ways to access countries where we did not, or had not, had a presence before. Four to five billion people who had not encountered the Jesus of the Bible lived in this band that stretched from Morocco to Malaysia. We had just left a country that had had a Christian presence since the 1700s and held the claim of the first church in West Africa. Knowing that we could not go back there, we began searching for the next assignment that God had planned for us. The idea of going to someplace where, as Paul stated, "the gospel had not been sowed," was indeed appealing. Being a part of this new wing, using unconventional ways to spread that seed was the refreshing change and challenge that we needed. As we looked at assignments from Afghanistan to Mongolia, we still had this desire to be in Africa, so we asked if they had any assignments there.

"Yes, there is one. In Sudan," came the reply.

Just that very name, the Sudan, conjured up a world of stories in my mind. Its history goes far back in time, including the biblical account of the "Ethiopian" eunuch. The country's name, *Sudan*, is a name given to a geographical region to the south of the Sahara, stretching from Western Africa to Eastern Central Africa. The name derives from the Arabic *bilād as-sūdān*, or "the lands of the Blacks." Its history begins in the eighth century BC when it was known as the ancient Nubian Kingdom of Kush. For much of that time, its capital was located in Meroë, about four hours north of the current Khartoum. There are still many prime pyramids standing there, and our family actually camped out among them one year.

There are several references to Kush and Nubia in the Bible, and one of the stories that has always fascinated me is the one about the Ethiopian eunuch. He was from Queen Candice's court, from the Kushite Kingdom, located predominately in present-day Sudan, as the pyramids and other historical artifacts attest to. He was not from the Kingdom of Aksum, which is present-day Ethiopia. The mis-translation came from a guy named Philostorgius back around 440 AD and has stuck around ever since.

It was not long after that initial conversation when we met David Garrison, who had recently done a vision trip into Sudan with another colleague, Robin, who would soon be our team leader. In his tiny office, David animatedly laid out all of his knowledge from his trip and what the possibilities looked like for getting into, and viably functioning in that land. To be fair, he didn't put that information on any bright and shiny silver platter. The vastness, harshness, barrenness, and unforgiving nature of simply living there was detailed.

NEW FRONTIERS: SUDAN (1993)

The people group we would be living among, the Beja, were a hard-as-dried-leather, nomadic people whose men spent their days roasting and drinking coffee—and keeping an eye on their camels. In fact, the Beja are the only known opposition to ever break a British fighting square. That happened during the conflict against British rule when the "Mahdi" took up arms against them, and the Hadendoa clan fought alongside him. There would be no one else from our organization in the country, so everything would be on our shoulders. Our team leader had lived there for some months but had since relocated to Kenya. He was to be our prime source of information and contacts inside the country. Much to our joy, about six months after we landed in Sudan another family joined us in the capital.

Chapter 11

SIDE TRIP

The road to Sudan had a curve in it, though, which went through Jordan. We had to learn Arabic to function in Sudan, so off to school we went. It was supposed to be two years, but that, too, had an interesting twist. By that time, our kids were in elementary school, so we had to find them appropriate ones to attend. April was enrolled in a British school, and Caleb went to a local Arabic language one. Caleb was only in Kindergarten 2 (KG 2), so for him to plunge into a school with a different language was not as big a challenge as it might have been for April. Plus, the location was close to our language school. The one thing we didn't know at that time was that he was dyslexic. We would notice that he would write his name in English from right to left and in Arabic from left to right—the opposite of what should be. So we knew there was an issue to be dealt with. At that time, residing in Jordan and Sudan, we didn't have a lot of corrective options. Initially we had no idea how we were messing him up. April never did have an Arabic language class, though about fifteen years later, while in university, she decided to return to Jordan for a summer term to study . . . Arabic!

Looking back over our time in Amman, we have often reflected on how it was the most challenging years of our time overseas. Each day was jam-packed: rise early to get kids ready for school, quickly review the day's lessons, get April in her taxi along with another classmate for the forty-five-minute ride to school, take Caleb with us, walk to school, drop Caleb off, take classes from 8 a.m. to 1 p.m., pick up Caleb after school, walk down the hill to meet with my tutor and practice language until late afternoon, get home for the kids by 3 p.m. (Kate), spend time with kids after school, eat dinner, put kids to bed, study the next day's lessons for two to three hours, sleep. Five days a week. It was exhausting, but ultimately, in the end, it was worth it. We learned the language. However, it was not in one straight shot. We had to do it twice, one year at a time.

Jordan was a great place to learn Arab culture and traditions. Yes, these vary from country to country and region to region, but Jordan/Syria/Lebanon are kind of like the Nebraska/Iowa/Kansas of Midwest America in these respects. Especially with the language. Middle of the road, easy to listen to, easier to learn than other dialects—at least *I* think so. The school we went to had great teachers whose Kingdom service in life was to train up their students to the highest standards possible. They did so with wonderful love and encouragement, right along with being tough taskmasters. I do clearly remember the first day of class when the man who started and ran the school told all of us newbies that it would take us about ten years to be comfortable with this language. Yikes! Not what one wants to hear on the first day. But I must confess, for most people that assessment is pretty accurate. Of course, there are always those rare students who hear something spoken once and are able to sear it into their brains' language files forever. Hated those people. Knew one guy who was reading *Swiss Family Robinson* in Arabic—for leisure—after only six months in the language! They make the rest of us look so feeble.

We each had our favorite teachers. Mine was, by far, Nellie. Over my two years of study, I had many classes with her as the tutor. She was a sweet mix of kindness, fun, and hard work. We ate meals at her house, got to know her family, and learned much more than just the Arabic language from her. Her cultural insights were rich and beneficial. Kate's favorite teacher was probably Basma, the one I was always afraid of because she was so strict. I avoided her classes until my last semester, and only then did I realize why Kate liked her so much. I regretted not having her more often. As with the others, they were all called by the Master to serve an important role in training up His servants to work in this part of the world.

They were often quite fun as well. I remember a story that one of them (Ghada) told us about how she always carried her big hat pins with her when she traveled by a service (pronounced ser-*veese*) taxi. These shared taxis traveled designated routes through the city and were a very economical way to get around. Because they would carry up to five passengers at a time, the passengers could be pretty close quartered in the rear seat. Every now and then a man's hand would start creeping in the wrong direction—but not for long. Those needles were a sharp and pointed reinforcement of the strict taxi etiquette rules that were not to be misused! Of course, the man could never utter a sound because he would be shamed for his indiscretion.

There were many cultural opportunities to experience in Jordan. The country was full of historical sites and architectural wonders of the ancient world. From Umm Qais in the north, to Jerash just north of Amman, to Petra and Wadi Rum in the south, the country has some unique opportunities to visit history. We certainly took full advantage of our times there and went just about everywhere we could. Right in the heart of Amman, every day I would walk by and often sit in and study on the steps of an ancient amphitheater. As I walked through those same streets practicing my Arabic, I would be in the shadow of the hilltop citadel, another ancient landmark that overlooks the whole city. And there was even the ancient Roman bath house that sits literally in the center of downtown that I passed by every single day—though at the time we lived there, it was not opened to the public yet. What a great place for our kids to grow up.

This upbringing led to one humorous incident a few years later when our family traveled to Rome for a holiday. One day we decided to take the kids to see the Colosseum, maybe one of the most famous architectural structures in the world. When we got inside the structure, Caleb blurts out, "Oh, just some more old rocks to see!" That was one of those, "Yes, and . . ." learning moments in their childhood education.

Because of school schedules, we often took family vacations during the months of July or August. April's birthday was in the first week of August, and after several years of these holiday seasons, April realized that she had spent her birthday in numerous different cities in Europe and the Middle East. Paris, Rome, Madrid, plus Greece, Germany, and Austria were all "birthday presents" for April while growing up. Greece was always one of her favorite places to visit.

Chapter 12

DENTISTS AND ARABIAN NIGHTS

During that first year of language study, I was blessed to meet a dentist by the name of Dr. Nayef Goussous. It was not because of his skills with teeth that we met, nor was he our family's dentist; rather, it was his amazing knowledge of ancient coinage. The first day that I walked into his circa-1950s dentist office and met the man behind the thick-rimmed glasses, I knew I would like him. Sitting there, surrounded by a flood of childhood memories brought on by his ancient equipment, I really didn't say much. I think I was just mesmerized by the jovial, slightly hunched over man who would, in the ensuing months and years, become not only my mentor in ancient coin collecting but my very dear friend as well.

He introduced me to the Jordanian world of the "Arabian Nights of coin collecting." There was seldom a day when visiting him at his office, which was stuffed in every corner with reference books about ancient coinage, that there would not be a new character come through his doors, asking his advice about a new find or trying to sell him a *special piece* that they had just come into possession of.

Abu Taksiim was the first that I was to meet. A quiet, gentle old man, somewhere in his eighties, always well-dressed and topped off with his immaculate white *hattah* or *ghutrah* (traditional headdress worn by men.) He and the doctor went way back in their friendship, and it was easy to see why. As they conversed with each other, there was always a sweet respect in the air. He often came into possession of some real special coins but never really did understand their significance or monetary value. The doctor did but was always fair with him, often making him accept more than what he was asking for the coins. Over time, I, too, purchased several items from him.

Abu Shadi was the next magical character I was to meet. A big, gregarious man with a huge Andy Devine smile, who I'm sure just came right out of the cave of the *Forty Thieves* the night before I first met him. This perception was enhanced one night when I went to his house in a nearby village. All manner of crusty-looking lads were darting about, seeming to say, "It's a good thing you are a friend of Abu Shadi." That very night he produced on the table in front of us, from every nook and cranny in his humble home, perhaps the single-largest collection of ancient coins I had ever seen (except the good doctor's). And, unlike the doctor's, these were all for sale.

There were several others in the days and months that would follow, many of whom the doctor would refer to as "crooks." Some even had names like "the Snake." He was always careful to alert me to various schemes that they would come up with to sell you something that was basically worthless. He was ever so patient in showing me how to recognize fakes, of which there were, and still are, an abundance of in the marketplace. Though I'm sure I have asked him the same question on numerous occasions, he never showed any degree of annoyance at my ignorance. He would always answer me as if it were the first time I had ever asked the question.

I have enjoyed countless hours in Nayef's home, looking at priceless treasures of the ancient world. Sometimes with a group of interested others, sometimes just him and me. Sometimes sitting at his kitchen table, balling up *mansef* (traditional Levantine dish made of lamb cooked in a sauce of fermented dried yogurt and served with rice or bulgur) in our fingers in between mentoring sessions. In the beginning his almost childlike glee when he would show me a unique coin caught me off guard. He would let me examine it while telling me the story of how he obtained it and then, with surprising speed, set the coin back down and move on to another coin with another story. I soon began to understand that, for Nayef, much of the joy was in the hunt. In the bargaining process. Coming into possession of something that few modern men have ever seen, let alone touched. The value; yes, that was all well and good. But the process of the collecting was where the rewards were to be found. It was a lesson well taught and one that I will ever be grateful for.

While in Jordan all three times, I was able to purchase many different coins, but one of my favorites was a widow's mite. There will always be the reminder of the story in the Bible about these coins being the smallest and least valuable of coins in Judea. Yet the widow gave all she had in honor to the Lord as opposed to the wealthy who gave only a small portion of what they possessed. There is a sharp contrast to the tetradrachms (an ancient Greek silver coin) that I have with the images of the wealthy leaders of Rome stamped on them.

When it came time for my family to leave Jordan, there was a deep sadness in my being; I didn't want our relationship to end. I wanted to pack Nayef up in my boxes and ship him to where we were headed. Sometimes it was difficult to accept the calling in my life—in times like this. I knew I was going where the Lord wanted me to be, but I also knew I was leaving a part of me behind. I am so grateful that since that initial departure, God has allowed me many more days and nights at the good doctor's house, pouring over excavated coins and other artifacts from the past, helping me to understand Near Eastern history with a depth I had never dreamed of. I only hoped and prayed that there would be many more, someday in the future.

Alas, it is the spring of 2021, and I find myself back in Amman, passing through once again. As usual, I give Nayef a call to set up a time to come and chat. The voice on the other end of the phone is a woman's—a kind lady that I had met several times before in his office where his ancient artifacts are now housed in the Ahli Bank Numismatic Museum. (She assisted Dr. Nayaf with all that went into setting up and running the museum. The research alone was staggering, and there was always a minimum of about fifty books piled in and around Nayef's desk. Some years ago, he gifted his collection to the government of Jordan for a museum where he acted as its curator.) It was a kind but sad voice on the other end of the line. She let me know that the good doctor was in a very bad way and was confined to his home. He had escaped death a couple of times before in the previous years, but this time it appeared he would soon be with his Maker. I would have loved to go see him one last time, but in the days of Covid, it was just not possible. I'm afraid that I'll have to wait until heaven for that encounter.

Since we were living in Jordan, we needed doctors and dentists for our family. The dentist we found would turn out to be one that we continued to use for the next thirty years! Even when we lived in other countries, we often passed through Amman for meetings, and each time we would make a visit to Dr. Shibley for a checkup and teeth cleaning. Just this past week, we paid him a visit for a teeth cleaning, and my wife had a look at our visits chart in the office. Twenty-eight years' worth of visits! Half of our time in the office was used just catching up on each other's children.

Prior to our family moving from Amman, April had braces put on her teeth by an orthodontist. We really struggled with the decision, as we knew we were going to be in Sudan shortly, and the best research we could find at that time said there was only one orthodontist in the country. To make this story shorter, we wound up sending April back to Jordan for her checkups (though probably not as regularly as would be the norm). Our daughter flew by herself from Sudan to Amman and back in a single day several times while she had her braces on. She would get on the plane in Khartoum in the morning and fly to Amman, where a friend would meet her and take her to the orthodontist. Then they would go shopping and buy the things we needed that we couldn't get in Sudan. The plane itself went on to Istanbul and then made its return through Amman and on to Khartoum. Our friend took April back to the airport in the afternoon to catch the return flight back to Khartoum. She was in eighth grade during this time. An interesting side note and a show of God's sovereignty is that very shortly after April stopped having to make those flights, the airline cancelled that routing!

Chapter 13

MOVING ON

Close to the end of our first year in language school, our team leader came to see us and ask if we would consider going into Sudan early. They needed someone on the ground ASAP, and he promised we could get in more language study in-country once we were in Khartoum. That was critical for us as we knew that one year of Arabic had us speaking at about a kindergarten level at best. Moving into Sudan where the dialect was quite different than the Levantine one we were learning was going to be tough. In fact, during our first few months in-country, we could hardly understand anyone when they spoke to us. The Sudanese are some of the fastest-speaking people in the Arab world, and their dialect is nearer to Egyptian in pronunciation. Think of getting on an Amtrack train in Chicago and hopping off one in Germany or France. Going from a rumbling ninety-kilometer-an-hour train to one that cruises along at three hundred kilometers an hour is immense. There is a noticeable difference!

The people themselves were kind and wonderful and are known throughout the Arab world as being the most gracious and hospitable. It was not unusual to be walking down a street and to be asked to come inside for a cup of tea or a cold glass of *karkadeh* (hibiscus tea). Making friends was easy, though there was always a subdued fear of the security forces there. No one trusted anyone else. They never knew if their brother or uncle or cousin was in the *maktab al am* (kind of like the FBI). The Northern Sudanese had what was called the "White House," remotely located in Juba, where people often *disappeared*, never to be seen again. During the civil war of 1983–2005, the Khartoum government used this as their primary torture site for anyone they thought was opposing them.[2] Most other torture houses were located out in the desert somewhere. I remember being told a story of a man who was taken into the desert to one of these houses. After being interrogated for some time, they told him he was free to go. Problem was, they were in the middle of the desert, and when you are blindfolded going in, you really have no idea where you are. Many, many people died in that desert while we lived there. Most simply got lost. In this case, the man left the house and, by the grace of God, found a road, and a vehicle came along and took him back to Khartoum.

Getting off the plane the first time in Sudan was the complete opposite of jumping into the cold waters of the Mediterranean. It was dry, dusty, and searing hot. When you breathe in that first breath after coming off an air-conditioned airplane, your lungs have to work extra hard to filter out the dust. It feels like you are sucking in the exhaust of the plane's jet engines. Thankfully our body temperatures are 98.6 degrees, and that must allow our windpipes to act as a cooling system on the way to the lungs. The outside

---

2. Peter Martell, "South Sudan's 'White House' - a House of Horrors," BBC News, Juba (July 4, 2011), https://www.bbc.com/news/world-africa-13995944.

temperature that first day was hovering at around forty-eight degrees centigrade (about 120 degrees Fahrenheit).

The very *first* time that Kate and I passed through Khartoum was in the mid-80s when we lived in Tanzania and were headed to Cairo. At that time there was some unrest going on in Sudan, and when the plane landed, the flight crew refused to get off. The new crew got on the plane, and off we went. Both of our memories go back to the stifling heat that we experienced while sitting on the tarmac and no AC going. Of course, there was also the question of whether we would be allowed to take off again. . . .

Because of the strained relationship between the US and Sudan in the last couple of decades, Americans were often looked on with much suspicion. There were not very many of us in the latter years of the old millennium. In fact, in the American school there was only our kids and one other American family's children. The rest were from all corners of the globe. Mostly children whose parents worked for an NGO or a diplomatic mission in the capital. This was a very good thing for our children as it was an important part of their expanding worldview. It was almost like being in a UN school for the nations. Relationships with American kids who haven't lived overseas has always been one of our children's main challenges when residing stateside. There were certainly plenty of benefits, like watching the giant tortoises saunter around the campus every day. I don't know exactly how much they weighed, but it was in the range of three hundred to five hundred pounds. We used to play softball on Saturday afternoons on the school grounds, and we always had *tortoise rules*. Running bases, fielding grounders, or catching fly balls could often be tricky when you were keeping one eye on the ball and the other on a slowly roaming tortoise.

One of our best friends in the country was our second landlord. He was a renowned doctor who eventually started his own hospital. We lived in one of his rental houses for several years, and when we left for a new assignment, we turned it over to another family that was moving to Khartoum. We left our house, vehicles, furniture, office, house girl, gardener, and dog to them and moved away to Nairobi with thirteen small boxes. We loved that house in Amaraat. Great location, good neighbors, and just the right size. It even came with Pitiful, our watchdog. Pitiful only had three fully workable legs—that's how he got his name. The fourth one was kind of cock-eyed at a strange angle. We never did know if that was from a neighborhood brawl or from a vehicle encounter. When the renters before us left the country, they took their dog far out of town (probably twenty miles away) and left him there. One day, after we had been in the house for a few weeks, he showed up like he owned the place. He just scaled the exterior security wall and came on in. My children will swear that he could leap up on the six- or seven-foot wall that surrounded our home in a single bound. I think he touched the wall on the way up, but he certainly did wind up on the top every time.

I first met Frank not long after arriving in town. We would become, and stay, good friends until we departed years later. Frank was the second-known Beja believer. He was a wisp of a guy. Stood about five feet nine and weighed maybe a hundred forty pounds with a few weights in his pockets. He spoke very broken English and was a good assistant to me in helping me adjust my Arabic dialect to that of the Sudanese. He was also instrumental in the discipling of new believers in Christ. He and Earnest* made a great team. Earnest was from a different tribe in the west of the country, but God somehow connected the two of them together, and they became quite a force during our years there. It was the two of them who helped establish the first group of believers in the East among the Beja.

My first trip to the coast was eventful. We drove for two days, stopping over in Kassala, about halfway between

Khartoum and Port Sudan, and spent the night in the Hipton Hotel. We were traveling with Donald, who was the first-known Beja believer and was blind. He had a great sense of humor and kept us continually entertained during our two-day trek. While at the hotel that evening, we went up on the roof to have dinner. One of the items on the menu was pigeon soup. Though that certainly did not sound appetizing to us (we had eggs,) Donald thought it sounded great. When it was finally served, the whole pigeon was in the bowl with the broth around it. My team leader and I just stared at it and began to silently chuckle. Donald picked up his spoon to enjoy his soup and stuck it in the bowl, then *thump, thump.*

"What is this?" he asked us with a quizzical look on his face.

Through our chuckles we replied, "That's your pigeon soup."

His now disgusted look only made us crack up even louder in the steamy, humid, Sudan night air. At least they had plucked the feathers off the bird.

Prior to heading out for the trip East, we all met together for a time of prayer. Our team leader had been out East before, but this was to be our first time. I would travel by road with him and Donald, and Kate and the kids would fly out after a few days. We were excited to see what would be our new hometown for the first time. During our prayer time our team leader had prayed specifically for a church clergy person who lived in our new town and was giving information to the government about the activities of foreigners who were Christians. It was very worrisome to him, and he asked God to help us deal with this person. He didn't want us hampered as soon as we arrived in town and were trying to establish the work there.

Once we arrived, we spent several days meeting people and establishing new relationships. On our last day in town before returning to Khartoum, we met with a Dinka believer named Meshack. He had lived there for many years and was a faithful servant of the Lord. As we sat down in the tiny ice cream shop to talk, our team leader asked Meshack how the clergyman was doing.

"Oh, you haven't heard?" replied Meshack.

"No, what?" asked our leader.

"Well, he was last seen leaving town about a week ago, headed for Khartoum, driving on the shortcut through the desert with several women along with him. They found their bodies, having gotten lost and died of thirst, a few days ago."

That really shook up our team leader as we recalled our prayer time just about one week before. Yet to Kate and me, we saw it as confirmation that God had a plan for us and wanted us in that town. He was going to take care of us in His own providential ways. This would be revealed to us many times while in Sudan.

About six months after we arrived in Khartoum, another family came to join us. We had been together in Amman studying Arabic the previous year, so our families already had a good start with our relationship. Elmer* and Minnie* had three boys when they arrived in Jordan and added a fourth one when they returned to Jordan a few years later. Shortly after they came in, our family moved to Port Sudan, where there was a central hub of Beja people living. Both Elmer and I worked for the same NGO and were working to assist the multitude of refugees and displaced people within the Sudanese borders.

Elmer had not yet had an opportunity to come and visit us in the East. He was heading up the work in Khartoum, and that kept him quite busy. We had been living in Port Sudan for many months, and I was going to make a trip to one of the more remote places where we had our relief work among the many displaced people in the country, and I encouraged Elmer to fly out and travel down to the site with me. It was about a fourteen-hour drive to reach the site, so we left at about 4 a.m. in order to arrive before dark. The day before I had let Frank and Earnest know that Elmer was in town, but they never showed up to greet him. I thought that very odd for this culture, and indeed it was.

We set out early and traveled about five or six hours until we reached what was usually a dry riverbed, only today it was a raging river that had formed due to heavy rains in the mountains the night before, and there was no way that we were getting across it. Nothing to do but to turn around and head back and try the next day to travel. Arriving home in the late afternoon, we decided to go and visit Frank and Earnest that evening in the displaced-persons camp where they lived and worked. The two of them had started meeting with a group of believers that had grown to about twelve people. They met each week in a different home, on a different day, and at a different time, as meetings of groups like this were illegal at that time. We thought it would be good to catch up with them and talk over how things were going. As we arrived to the pieces of metal, canvas, and cardboard that was the home of Earnest's mother, we were greeted like we were ghosts. A thoroughly frightened mother quickly dragged us inside with her fingers to her lips, indicating to be quiet. What unfolded in those next tense minutes was the story of how the security forces, AKs in hand, had come to the recent meeting of the believers, surrounded the place, and taken Frank and Earnest, as well as the others, into custody. Frank and Earnest would be held for thirty-seven days while being interrogated and beaten daily. At least now we knew the reason that they hadn't come to greet us the day before.

She explained to us that we needed to leave quickly as the security people were at the end of the road, watching her place. Sure enough, when we walked out to our vehicle, there at the end of the dirt road was a motorcycle with two security men eyeing us. By now our hearts were thumping loud enough to be heard by the whole neighborhood, and as we got into our vehicle to leave, they promptly hopped on their motorcycle and followed us. We quickly devised a plan to make this look like we were simply on a work-related mission, as both of these men worked for our NGO. We slowly drove over to where our wood-shacked office was located and talked with the night guard there, inquiring where the manager was. When we pulled into the front of the office, the motorcycle stopped at the end of the road and waited—and watched. Our fears rose as the minutes passed by.

Leaving the office, we decided to continue on to the manager's house in another section of the very large camp. The roads leading to his place were very maze-like, designed for donkey carts, and I knew them well from working in the area for so long. I knew of a particular junction where one road panned out into about five different others, and if we weren't seen, we could lose our tail. This time as we pulled away from the offices and passed by the security men who were trying their best to be inconspicuous, I sped up and headed into the road maze. Sure enough, we were able to lose them, and we continued on to the manager's house. Not knowing if his house was being watched as well, we talked with him in a normal way, out in the street, and explained the situation. From there we knew we needed to head back to our house where my wife and kids were. I had a lot of fear that security was already there, and there was no telling what was going on. So about five minutes into our return, we stopped in a dry riverbed and prayed. I had to stop as my foot was bobbing up and down on the gas pedal out of fright. We asked the Lord for wisdom in the situation, protection for my family, and safety for Frank and Earnest. Finally my leg stopped shaking, and we returned to the house.

Once home we had a burn party. Lots of *unneeded* documents went up in smoke that evening. We had no idea if we would be paid a visit sometime soon by security, so better safe than sorry. The one regret was that we had to destroy a video of a baptism that we had performed some weeks before on Earnest's sister. It was a beautiful setting in the Red Sea with Earnest on one side and me on the other. From that day forward, I never did another baptism in the country. But Frank and Earnest did a multitude of them. I had trained them both and told them it was now their responsibility going forward.

What we later found out was that one of the young ladies who had been part of the group and had been baptized was found out by her family. This led to a series of threats and punishments from her family. She eventually could not take it anymore and told the local authorities the details of where and when the meetings took place.

Life continued on as normal for several months after that incident. Frank and Earnest were released after the thirty-seven days in custody, thanks to the persistence of our NGO project manager who continually pestered the security folks where they were detained. He was told on numerous occasions not to interfere or come back as it didn't concern him, but he was undeterred. He let them know that we knew where they were being detained, and I think that fear of the outside world possibly coming to a knowledge of this incident was instrumental in their eventual release.

When I finally heard that they had been released, I went back out into the camp to see them. Frank was in so much pain from the beatings that he could not get up out of his bamboo bed to greet me. Feebly he reached his arm up around my bent over body and said in an octave barely above a whisper, "God was so good to us." It was all I could do not to let the waterfall of tears come rushing down my cheeks. In the hours that followed, he and Earnest unfolded their days in captivity—the first three of them being made to stand upright in a courtyard in the blazing one-hundred-twenty-degree heat, while getting physically and verbally abused. I don't think Frank's kidneys ever did function properly after those beatings. Earnest came out a bit better with only a punctured eardrum as a long-term effect. The good news is that both of them continued on in their service to the King, though they eventually went down separate paths. Over the years Frank spent even more months in prison for his faith, and Earnest traveled extensively around the country, planting new work and discipling new believers.

We fully expected to be asked to leave within days after this incident, but life continued on as normal as normal can be for some months. Kate's parents came for a visit and got to experience where we lived and the people we were around. Our projects continued to function and flourish. We were involved with several different community health and education programs out in the camps. Brick making, water supplying, reading and writing classes were all part of what our NGO was involved in. All were much needed for the hundreds of thousands who were located in the IDP (internally displaced persons) camp—which was actually one of the largest in the world at that time. We also had a camp located fourteen hours south of us, which was much smaller but in equally dire need of help. That camp brought with it several particularly challenging obstacles and issues. Due to its location, it was difficult to get any supplies to it. There was no other option other than the long overland trek, and that was always an adventure. At different times we got caught in blinding dust storms (*haboobs*), stuck in quicksand-like mud, and stopped by raging *wadis* (dry riverbeds that flash-flooded). There was one time when we had traveled about five to six hours south when a security patrol stopped us in a three-building village. They *requested* we use our vehicle to take a wounded man back to a clinic three hours in the opposite direction. I was pretty sure there was no clinic in that six-building village, but I agreed when they brought out this young man who had three bullet holes in him and was bleeding excessively. They said he was a thief whom the police had shot while trying to steal something. To me it appeared that he would not even make the trip back, but they were confident he would.

When we pulled up to said village and found out there was no clinic there, they requested I continue on back to Port Sudan. I firmly but politely refused. When we had taken the young man out of my vehicle, it was covered in a pool of blood that had to be at least a third of what the human body holds. They set him on the ground, and he promptly fell over. With every pump of his heart, blood shot out from his wounds. I reasoned with the police that the man would never make it further on the desert roads and that I needed to travel another nine to ten hours that day to reach my destination. I had done what they had asked of me and now needed to be on my way. They agreed and allowed us to carry on.

When I finally reached our camp that evening, I had one of our workers help me clean out the, by now, dried blood on the way-back carpet. The flies were swarming in a frenzy as we labored to scrub the carpeted flooring. We spent three hours scrubbing (and several more hours once we returned home) to get it somewhat clean and smell-free. On the trip home several days later, I stopped by the police checkpoint in the village I had picked him up at and inquired about the young man, fully expecting them to inform us of his death. Much to our surprise, they told us he made it back to Port Sudan alive and was now in custody there. I'm quite sure he needed several transfusions to replace all the blood he lost, and I'll never again underestimate the strength in a person who has a will to live.

That was not to be our only challenge associated with that camp in the south. When we first started our work there, we had placed a young man, whom we believed was a Christ-follower, in the position of director. For the first six months or so he did a pretty good job running and managing the facilities and programs we were carrying on there. Most were educational in scope, but there was also some disaster relief distribution as well. We paid the director a good salary with solid benefits, but apparently that was not enough. At about the six-month point of his employment, he sent a letter to me saying that he knew what we were really doing (telling people about Jesus), and that if we did not give him a huge raise in salary, he was going to go to the authorities and tell them all about us. Mild panic set in with me, and I immediately called in Frank and Earnest and asked them what they thought we should do.

Neither of them seemed as worried as I was, and after talking through the situation, we went up to the roof of our building and had a time of intense prayer. We asked God to help us to listen to Him and to guide our thoughts and actions in a way that would be glorifying to Him. That gave me great comfort, and I sent a reply to the director saying that we could talk about the situation the next time he was in town. That did not seem to satisfy him, and about a month later, I got another letter from him stating that if I didn't give him a certain, very large, sum of money when he arrived in town a few days later, he would turn us in to the security people. Now the real panic set in. I called Frank and Earnest over again, showed them the letter, and enquired as to what they thought we should do. This was a real threat as they had, by this time, gathered a group of believers together, and they would certainly be exposed by this young man. Again, we had a very intense time of crying out to God. I remember telling Him that we did not know what we should do and asking Him to show us what it was that we needed to do. While I would like to say this calmed my heart, I confess that I was still strung with stress over the impending situation. Oh, me of little faith.

Three days later Frank and Earnest came over to our house and asked me if I had heard the news. I had not. The director was on his way up to town and got sick along the way. When he arrived in town, they put him in the hospital, and he promptly died. Now it was my time to be in awe and fear of the Lord. To Frank and Ernest, this was no big deal. Their response to this was a simple one and one I would equate to some of the early biblical stories. They told me in a Psalms 138:8 matter-of-fact way, "He tried to mess with God's plan, and God took care of him." It was the judgment of God. End of story. It was very much like the Ananias and Sapphira story in the book of Acts. I was so impressed with their response to this that that very hour is etched in my memory for eternity. That was twice since we had committed to go to that town that God directly intervened to reassure us that He was sovereign and in control of every situation. We would be there for as long as He desired.

In the months following the house arrest of all the believers, we were able to renegotiate a new operational contract for our NGO with the government. It was a long and arduous task, but, in the end, it gave us a satisfying relief of three more years of assisting the community and working with the leaders we were mentoring. It turned out to be short lived. Three days after signing the new contracts, local government officials, on behalf of the central government in Khartoum, came to our project office and closed us down.

"Mick, you need to come to the project right now. The government officials are there, and they are confiscating everything and shutting the project down."

I couldn't believe what I was hearing. I had spent months in negotiations, and everyone was very pleased with the work we had been doing up to this point. Our water supply program was particularly crucial to the camp populace as there was no other means of getting fresh water in the camp. We had a couple of tractors with trailers attached that had huge water tanks on them. We made two or three trips each day to a government water supply point some miles away, where we loaded the tanks and took the water to our office in the camps. There we distributed it into twenty-liter containers that the people brought. Sometimes the lines could be hundreds of people long. Without us there would be no water. It just didn't make any sense. Not much of the next two to three months made any sense—until about eighteen months later.

Once I arrived at our offices and had discussions with the officials, who were carrying out their orders handed down from above, I got the feeling that this might be the beginning of the end of our time in Port Sudan. They even tried to confiscate my vehicle, but I refused and told them it was a personal vehicle, and they could not have that. (In the end, two months later, the governor of the state was seen driving it.) Even though it is common for NGOs to make agreements with governments whereby they get all the project assets when a project is completed, I never did understand how a government could just come in with no explanation and take away everything that an organization owned, prior to completion, but I have seen it happen over and over again during our years overseas.

It was shortly after that when I got a call from my colleague in Khartoum, informing me that we had thirty-six hours to pack up and leave the country. I told him that was impossible, and he was able to plead with the authorities to give us five days to sell all we owned and drive to Khartoum where we would get our exit visas to leave the country. Turns out it took the government about five *weeks* once we arrived in the capital to get the paperwork done to allow us to leave!

On our last Sunday in town, we decided we should go to one of the local churches that we often attended and say our goodbyes. It was a sad time for everyone. What made it even sadder was that when we returned home that evening, we found our house had been broken into. Stuff was scattered everywhere, indicating they were looking for something in particular. Since they left our computers and other personal belongings untouched and took all the money in the house, we were pretty confident about what they were after. The saddest part of that is that the money they took was for the salaries of the workers on our project. The only thing they seemed to leave behind was some bloody handprints, probably from scaling the wall to get in. The odd part was that the only way for them to get in was through our neighbor's yard—but no one claims to have seen or heard anything. And, of course, nothing was ever recovered.

That was a tough time on everyone. The kids cried, we cried, we prayed, and in those last days we had a fire sale for our home furnishings. We loved that small town on the coast with the warm friends we had made among the Beja and other Sudanese. We especially loved having a job that allowed us to help hundreds, if not thousands, every day in that large IDP camp.

Our house was a big old Sudanese coastal home designed to get whatever breezes were around from whatever direction they were coming from. Originally designed in a U shape with a courtyard in the middle, it was redesigned to close in the courtyard, thereby doubling the size of the house. It was so spacious that when we first moved in, I would get on my bicycle and chase the kids on their rollerblades around the center of the interior walls. Various other ball games also ensued on a regular basis. The windows in each room opened both on the inside and the outside walls (originally for the breeze to pass through), and when they were open, it made the house feel even more expansive. There were glass panes as well as shutters on each window, and undoubtedly those shutters saved many a broken glass. Because electricity was so sporadic, we had a generator to keep the fridge and fans going.

It is said that Port Sudan, along with Masawa and Djibouti, are three of the hottest places on the planet, especially during the summer months. During the night we would run the air conditioner in our bedroom, and the whole family would sleep in there. We had a waterbed that stayed so warm that we had to soak our sheets with cold water to sleep on it. The very strange thing was that the thermometer that we had told us our bedroom was cooled down to eighty-five degrees, yet when we walked inside it from the main rooms it felt like we were walking into an igloo. Our water tank storage was on the roof, and in the summer we had to get cool water out of the hot water heater, which was in our bathroom (that we never turned on). If we tried to use it straight from the pipes, it would scald us. The temperature would often be fifty degrees centigrade outside (126 degrees Fahrenheit), and with the humidity it was quite brutal. So much in fact that most of the residents would leave the town from May to October. Even most of the Beja went up into the nearby mountains for the summer.

We had a variety of pets in that house—dog, cat, desert tortoise. One time we were traveling on the tarmac road from Khartoum, and we found a young, giant tortoise ambling along the desert road. Since it was not yet fully grown and only weighed about forty pounds, we took him home and let him roam around our yard where he had a good supply of grass to graze on. I wonder what the government did with him when we left? We also had our friendly neighborhood dumpster-diving camel that would enjoy whatever he could find in the one located just outside our side road. Camels were everywhere in town and were integral to the Beja culture. They almost enjoyed the same reverence that people give to their cattle in India.

One of the fun things we liked to do as a family was go to the local *souk* (market) in both Khartoum and Port Sudan. When we would go there, I would always be looking for old relics of the Sudanese culture—swords, shields, coins, knives, wooden boxes, or spears—while April loved to scour the boxes and boxes of beads that they sold there. By the time we left the country, she had quite a collection that she took back to the States with her. I especially remember the huge amber beads that had hung around some grandmother's neck decades ago and commanded a much heftier price than many of the others. I know that there are some of those in our storage boxes somewhere. There are certainly plenty of aged tools of warfare that are waiting for me to hang on some wall.

Our family often had the occasion to travel between Khartoum and Port Sudan. It was a long journey, usually beginning around 4 a.m. and seeing us on the other end by nightfall. There was a curfew during those days in Khartoum, and nighttime travel was prohibited, so we worked within those parameters. On rare occasions we stayed the night in the Hipton Hotel in Kassala, which was about halfway. Kassala was a fascinating little town and the very unofficial capital of the Beja. It was kind of a crossing point in and out of Ethiopia. The market in Kassala was quite lively. It was one of the main places to purchase Beja swords. Every Beja man had one. They were between three and four feet long and sharp as razors. Many were made out of old railroad spikes and other discarded pieces of hardened steel. Most came with a leather sheath fashioned by the Beja leather workers. From time to time, you could find very old swords that had seen their share of battles from years past. The old swords, passed down from one generation to the next, had grooves along the sides that allowed air in while removing them from their sheathes. This made them faster to draw and ensured they wouldn't get stuck. As mentioned, our house in the States has a nice collection of these beautiful examples of Beja craftsmanship. It was fun to watch the men judge how good the steel was by holding the sword in the air and jerking their wrists to make the blade shake. It was in this manner they decided if it was a worthy purchase or not.

Beja shields were another, much rarer, artifact of generations past. The shields were made of elephant skin and brought from Southern Sudan. The elephant skin was folded over many times, making the shield sturdy but still somewhat light. The handle, also made of elephant skin, was tied on with giraffe skin. A piece of metal was overlaid in the center to prevent swords from stabbing through. I saw less than five of these during our years there. In our latter years, I was finally able to obtain one of them that serves as a historical reminder of how very hard and tough the Beja culture is, and that toughness extends into the presenting of Truth to a people who have had it hidden from them for centuries.

On the days when we decided to travel from one end to the other in one long day, usually about fourteen hours, we would stop at the only "tree" along that desert road. It was more like a giant bush, but it did provide a small amount of shade, which in 110-plus-degree sunshine was very welcoming. It was there where we would always enjoy a fresh watermelon. From that very first time stopping there, that tree was always called the watermelon tree, and we never failed to stop under it, coming or going.

On our first drive to Port Sudan as a family, we had to bring along the cat that we had acquired while in Khartoum. We decided to drug it so that it would sleep during the long trip and not be freaking out all over the vehicle. Well, it worked . . . kind of. What happened was that it just made him groggy, and he spent a good part of that trip yowling and weaving all over the vehicle. We never knew what a drunk cat looked like until that adventure.

Chapter 14

TAKING A BREATHER

One of the blessings of living on the edge of the Red Sea was the pristine waters that cozied up to the coastline. We took advantage of those waters every chance we got. We quickly made friends with a German man who ran a diving company. Harry was a single guy who was a dive instructor and tried to make a go of it running dive trips in one of Jacque Cousteau's former playgrounds. Some of the most memorable dives I have experienced in my life were off that coast. Pristine, clear water in which you could see a dime at eighty feet. That was where Caleb and April both had their first diving adventures. Caleb was about seven and April was nine when we went out to one of the colorful reefs one weekend. Caleb loved the diving; April did not. It would be several more years before Caleb could legally get his open water dive certification, but he enjoyed every opportunity when Harry would take him down and buddy-dive with him. April, on the other hand, has never again put on a breathing apparatus for under the water. Thankfully, however, she does enjoy snorkeling these days.

Harry's boat was nothing special, maybe twenty-four feet in length, and had seen many a day in the water, but it was a great boat for our family to spend a day out in the Red Sea. One of those days, after enjoying the beauty of the local reefs, we headed back in during the latter part of the afternoon. About an hour and a half out of the port, the boat suddenly sprung a leak. A serious leak. One that required all of us to hastily and hurriedly start bailing out the water with anything we could get our hands on. It seems that the bilge pump was not functioning, and it was going to be up to us to keep that boat afloat.

About thirty minutes out, we began to question whether we were going to make it back. All of us were good swimmers, and we had life jackets and BCs (buoyancy compensators) to keep us above water if things didn't work out, but the prospect of being that far from shore as the sun was going down was not an appealing one. I cannot remember a dive when I didn't see sharks off that coast. Big sharks—hammerheads, black tip reef sharks, and others with menacing looks to them. Sharks rarely bother people who are diving, but they become quite curious when something is flopping around on the surface of the sea. It's amazing what goes through one's mind at a time like that. Needless to say, we made it back to the port, and Harry's boat lived to make many more dive trips.

Chapter 15

THE BEJA

As we had come to Port Sudan to work among the Beja people, we felt it was important to try and learn their customs and cultural ways. One of the prime daily tasks of Beja men and women is making coffee. And not the *light brown water* most Americans identify as coffee. This stuff was as thick as mud and just as dark. This posed an interesting dilemma for me as I was not a coffee drinker. In fact, I never remember drinking coffee before moving to Port Sudan. Kate has reminded me that there were possibly a few times during my language study in Amman that I imbibed with my language tutor—and she may be correct; I just remember drinking tea while there. But since this was a very important custom in their daily life, I felt it my duty to participate.

So, one day I decided to sit down outside my front door with Ali, our house guard/worker. Ali didn't know a single word of English, so sitting down on the ground with him for the two-to-three-hour ritual of coffee making and drinking was really going to help my Arabic improve. Plus, I was going to learn how to drink coffee. The Beja drink their coffee in small little teacups that amount to barely two or three good sips of the nectar. They also add in copious amounts of sugar to make it sweet enough to be drinkable. The bottom half of the cups are usually not drinkable due to the *sludge* of the coffee grounds mixed with sugar. The process itself is fascinating as it includes everything from roasting, grinding, and cooking the beans over a tiny three-stone fire.

A few hours later, after drinking the higher end of the customary three to five cups, I had learned a lot about that Beja custom. About twelve hours later, after bouncing off walls and frantically rushing around my house and job all day, I made sure I never again drank five cups. I would not recommend to anyone to make drinking Beja coffee your first coffee-drinking experience. But I honestly believe that first time together with Ali was an important stepping stone in our relationship. Later on we were blessed to be invited to go up into the mountains where his family lived, and we spent some days with them in their village. And that's a whole other story.

We had asked Ali about visiting his family clan up in the mountains around Sinkat on several occasions without much response. Then one day, out of the blue, came his invitation. Off we went, not knowing what to expect at all. It took us a few hours to reach his home village, which was not very large. Basically, the Beja are a nomadic people grouped into five tribes and occupying mountain country between the Red Sea and the Nile and from Egypt to Eritrea. Numbering about four million in the early twenty-first century, the Beja are descended from peoples who have lived in the area since 4000 BCE or earlier.

Many of the Beja speak Tobedawi, a Cushitic language, and some who are further south speak Tigre. There are also many who speak Arabic, as that is the common language of the Northern Sudanese. Christianity was common among them in the sixth century, but since the thirteenth century many have been nominally Muslim. The Beja, by and large, prefer to live somewhat separated from their neighbors, and many care very little about trade unless it is with other Beja. Having lived around and among them, I can certainly confirm that modernization is not one of their attributes.

The Beja are predominantly pastoralists, migrating their goats, camels, and flocks over immense distances and living almost entirely off of their milk, butter, and meat. Lineage is traced through the father's line, and their relationships are very similar to that of Arab culture. Under Muslim law, Beja men can have many wives, but typically only the wealthy choose this. There are cultural expectations in marriage, including that a man should marry his paternal uncle's daughter, and he is to provide a dowry of livestock to the bride's family. Boys are circumcised, usually within a few days of birth, and girls are subjected to clitoridectomy any time before the age of nine.[3]

The couple of days we spent with Ali's clan were fascinating. While drinking copious amounts of coffee, we sat around in their small huts (made from straw mats laid over a wooden frame) and talked—or better said, *listened*. Because they mostly talked in Tobedawi, we didn't understand much of anything, though we did have someone translating to us in Arabic. Then again, we had less than two years of Arabic learning at that point, and I'm quite sure that there were many misunderstood conversations.

Since the male and female members of the clan are strictly separated, I was hanging around with the guys while Kate was with the women. The kids went wherever they wanted. We had some interesting experiences to share with each other when that weekend was over that were very

---

3. Britannica, written and fact checked by the editors of Encyclopedia Britannica article history. Revised and updated by Amy McKenna.

valuable to our cultural understanding of the Beja. Kate remembers the kids spending a lot of time up on the roof rack of our vehicle, where they slept at night. Kate and I slept in our tent. The Beja slept in their huts.

Chapter 16

THE KIDS' SCHOOLING

Our kids really loved living in Port Sudan. It was a very small community, and it didn't take long for everyone in town to realize that there was a *Khawaja* (foreigner) family living there. Since we were the only White family living there at that time, it was very easy to recognize us. It would have been totally impossible for one of our children to get lost for more than two minutes. Much of our time in Africa was similar, and, as a result, our children had a huge amount of freedom to move about in the communities and towns we resided in. Major crimes were very scarce (except during the civil wars), and even minor crimes like theft were quite few. I believe that is one of the sweet benefits of living in community, as opposed to our Western individualistic ways that are prevalent in America.

Because there was not a school with a good Western curriculum, and the kids were still a bit young for boarding schools, Kate and I made the decision to homeschool the kids. I helped out where I could (taking them on field trips to see camels or going with me to work), but most of the teaching landed on Kate's shoulders. Good thing she had an MS in education! The trouble was, she found out after one year of teaching that she really didn't like teaching all that much. What we wound up doing was getting their core subjects done in the mornings and then taking them to the "sister school" for the afternoons. That way they could learn what they needed to and yet still have a great segway into the local kids' culture from the sister school. That school, located in the center of town, was run by Catholic nuns and had been there for many years by the time we rolled in.

At first the kids were quite hesitant about going to a school that was only in Arabic, but they soon adjusted to that. What they weren't so sure about were the disciplinary actions of the teachers. It was very soon after they began attending that, while they didn't know the names of all their teachers, they knew them by the type of *instrument* they meted out discipline with in their classrooms. There was the *hose* teacher, the *ruler* teacher, the *cane* teacher, and on down the line. Each day they would come home with stories about the local students that got smacked that day for classroom indiscretions. Then finally one day, Caleb came home beaming. When we inquired why he was so happy, he gleefully replied, "I got beat today!" You see, for Caleb that was his unofficial acceptance into that culture/community. He was now *one of them*. April, on the other hand, would have been mortified to ever get whacked in school. She was not at all worried about being part of that gang.

We were very blessed during those early days to have other team members come and join us, though they did not live in-country at that time. Most lived and worked with the Beja clans who lived in Southern Egypt. Some of them are still plodding along, planting and watering seed, and being faithful to the call among the Beja people that so few people on this planet have ever heard of. One couple and their children have lived and worked among them for two decades now and have seen some amazing heart transformations, with groups of them meeting together to study the Word. I am confident that one day, when my time is finished on this earth, I will have the great joy of seeing many Beja in heaven, praising the name of Jesus.

Chapter 17

JORDAN: PHASE II (1996)

After being "asked to leave" the country, we made the decision to return for another year of Arabic study in Jordan. We had only gotten one year of formal study, and we both knew we needed a deeper knowledge of the language. So back to school we went.

Like the first year, it was tough. But having those extra few years already in Jordanian and Sudanese cultures, where Arabic was spoken, was helpful in that transition. We were familiar with the city and had some friends that we returned to, but we had some real soul searching going on during that year. Neither of us felt like God was calling us away from Sudan, like He did from Sierra Leone. We knew we needed to go back, even though all of our leadership told us that our days in Sudan were finished.

Chapter 18

STATESIDE

Following that year of Arabic study, we were due for some time stateside, and a lot of things unfolded during that year. We took some time on the way to the States to travel through Southern Europe, and that was refreshing. We got Eurorail passes for the family and train-hopped all over the place. I remember once, when Kate and I were traveling alone some years earlier, while waiting for a train connection in Southern Spain that was to take us to Madrid, another train came along headed to Portugal. So we just jumped on that one, and off we went. I'm sure that a great part of our family's love for trains comes from our European travel adventures over the years.

Once stateside, we got our kids into good schools, reconnected with some people who had been supporting us, and continued the process of evaluating all that had happened and where we sensed God leading us in the next season of life. Sudan would not leave the picture.

That year of schooling for the kids was quite different. We did some testing on Caleb and confirmed what we suspected—he was dyslexic. We were able to get him into a school that specialized in working with young children with learning challenges, and he had a banner year. We had held him back a year in school due to his needs, and by the end of the year, he had jumped back up to his normal grade level. April, on the other hand, did not fare so well. We put her into a good Christian school and thought she would really enjoy the *normalcy* of American education. How wrong we were. By the end of the year, she swore she did not ever want to come to America again. It took her months to find a good close friend that she could share things with. She had no idea what a clique was until she went to that school. Living overseas, kids tend to be much more transient, and as they move around from country to country, they learn to not take a lot of time sorting out who they want to be friends with. They all know that everyone is different, so that becomes the norm and something to uncover and celebrate. When April started school in Khartoum the following year, she had more than half a dozen life-long friends in a matter of days from the beginning of the school year. As a general rule, there is no one who "doesn't fit" in their schools, so inclusivity is simply the accepted thing to do. Certainly not so in schools in America, as April found out the hard way. Yes, she had a few *closer* friends, yet at the same time there were certainly *exclusions* in their classes.

Each time we returned to the States for a time of renewal, visiting with family and friends and getting some more training, we also spent a fair amount of time in speaking engagements. While iterating the stories of what God had been doing in each of the locations He had placed us in, we often told some humorous stories about our children as they grew up being *third culture kids* (TCKs). They hated that. Even more so when they were asked to come to the front and stand up with us. What was even worse was when they had to go into Sunday school classes for their age group and were often asked to tell their own stories or to answer questions about living in Africa. April once told us about this one: "One time a teacher asked me in a Sunday school class [eighth grade] how long it took us to drive to Africa. My prompt response was that it took about three days, and we would take the 'under-the-ocean highway' and drive straight through! I let her think that for all of the class time until Caleb made me feel guilty, and I told her I was just joking at the end of class." Dumb questions get dumb answers. . . .

And the things people would ask us!? There were other stories that we remember hearing them tell groups of adult listeners, like the one about their pet python snake that they allowed to sleep under their bed each night. Kate and I got quite a laugh when we overheard Caleb expounding on that one.

Chapter 19

GOD'S SOVEREIGNTY (1998)

About four or five months into Kate and my time in the States, we got a call from a colleague who was working on some projects in Sudan. He didn't live there, but he traveled in and out and had made a lot of contacts. One of them was a government official in the sports world, and it turns out they needed someone to help their country improve their sports programs. Our heart rates rose, and the next thing you know, I was on a plane to Khartoum to meet with a multitude of government people involved with sports. Because I had coached tennis and basketball and had played half a dozen other sports in my life, and I now worked for a sports development company, I appeared to be a perfect fit for what they were looking for. But there was this glitch. Only eighteen months before, the government had asked me to leave the country, apparently never wanting me there again. Now it was clearly God's time to once again show His sovereignty over this dilemma. I remember my team leader telling me that if I ever tried to get back into this country, I would be arrested immediately.

The whole flight there my emotions were running wild. I had gotten a visa, and that was a major thing back in the day, so surely they knew I was coming. When they heard me speak Arabic, they would recognize that I spoke their dialect, and when I engaged in their unique greetings, they would know I had lived there before. What would happen when they started checking up on me? Would we be kicked out again? Would all of this just be a temporary assignment where we uprooted our kids once again? Would we come away from this even more discouraged? I would probably know at least some of these answers as I walked off that plane onto the one-hundred-twenty-degree desert tarmac at the airport.

As we were disembarking and I reached the exit door at the top of the portable stairs, I could hear a rather stern man at the bottom of the stairs, asking each of the men ahead of me if they were *Mick*. As I surveyed the situation, I noticed that everyone was getting onto two large buses to the left of the stairs. There was one smaller bus to the right that no one was getting on. When I reached the bottom, and the man asked me if I was *Mick*, I replied affirmatively. At that point he told me to follow him, and he and I marched over to the bus on the right. Once on the bus, I was asked for my passport and luggage tickets. It was at that point that my former team leader's words rang very loudly in my ears: *If you ever try to go into that country again, you'll be arrested*. Resigned to my fate, and trusting my Master, I obediently followed onto the small bus. As the other two larger buses rumbled off to the right side of the main terminal, our bus promptly headed off in the other direction. It was at this point I began to think of the biblical stories of Paul's prison experiences.

Well, it turns out that I was on the VIP bus and was headed to a special terminal where I was told to sit down, have some tea, and wait while the entry formalities were taken care of. Within fifteen minutes, my luggage miraculously appeared, along with my stamped passport, and we were off to my hotel. It should be said that the normal time for that procedure well exceeded an hour in those days. From that point and for the next five days, I was ushered around the city, meeting one important official after another, from government ministers to the head of Parliament. It quickly became clear that God had orchestrated this trip to reassure me that it was He who was in charge of our destiny. It would be He who would put His protective cover on our family and allow us to glorify His name while here.

When it came time for me to return stateside, the minister of sports didn't want me to leave. I had to explain to him that I had work obligations in America but that I would return with my family by the summertime. What followed was many years of effective service for the King.

Chapter 20

RAMADAN

Having already been through several Ramadans, I was constantly being asked about Christian fasting practices by the locals. They would always tout how this special month, required by their religious tenants, brought them closer to God, and they asked why I didn't fast too. Trying to explain how and why we Christians fasted had very little effect on them, since it was something that was individually based and not community based. From what I had already observed, I was pretty sure I didn't want to enter into the kind of fasting that brought out so much anger and cheating and so many other undesirable character traits that did not seem to be the norm for their daily lives.

However, one year I decided that I would fast through the month of Ramadan—though I did not tell them what I was doing—so that I would never *not* have an answer to their constant badgering about how tough it was. The hardest part was the twelve-hour shift—kind of like moving to the opposite side of the world—that the body had to adjust to.

There was plenty of eating going on, only it was during the nighttime hours. No one was starving. In fact, a large number of people gain weight during this month. Very little work is carried on during the day; add the large consumption of food during the nights, and that adds up to added kilos. Unlike them, I did drink water during the day, as not doing so was simply not wise in a land where temperatures soared over one hundred degrees most days.

Ever since that time, I have been able to honestly reply to the charge of, "You just don't understand what it's like fasting through Ramadan." I do understand its challenges, but I still do not comprehend the built-up aggression that is often displayed during the latter weeks of that season.

Chapter 21

CAMELS, CAMPING, AND CULTURE

One of the fun things our family did while living in Sudan was go camping in the desert. And since most of Northern Sudan is desert, that left us quite a range of places to go. We had one spot that was probably our favorite. It was a rock outcropping maybe half a kilometer off the main road, heading north out of Khartoum. We would pick up some firewood from vendors on the side of the road just outside of town and load it up on our roof racks. In about an hour and a half, we would turn off that road and head for our hidden campsite behind those rocks. We went there often with friends who had kids about the same age as ours and just spent time doing nothing but talking and laughing, while the kids played like mountain goats on the large rocks. It was also the place where my children learned to drive. We just plopped them down behind the steering wheel and told them to watch out for rocks jutting out of the ground. Off they would go, out into the vast expanse of desert that was their driver's education course. From the beginning, it was always April who had the lead foot and Caleb who was the more cautious one. Still true to this day. By the time both of them were twelve or thirteen, they were pretty good behind the wheel. And it was a stick shift!

Camels can be a finicky animal at times—like, most of the time. We had several opportunities to ride them out in the desert. There were almost always some eager Beja people roaming around with their herds who were glad to accept a small donation to have a laugh at some crazy *khawajas* (foreigners) wanting to show off their expertise on a camel. On one particular day, the trash talking heated up, and it was decided that a race should take place among the bravado. Let it be said that I was not part of that challenge. I had ridden my share of camels over the years and didn't feel the need to give the Beja even more to laugh about. Anyway, there was this one camel that decided the guy on his back, a teacher at the American school in Khartoum, was not someone he liked. He continually tried to bite him until the guy jumped off and declared himself a non-participant. There was another similar time when a group of us were riding camels in the desert when this one guy, who was riding a racing camel and did not know it, had the ride of his life. It was like watching a bucking bronco in the Calgary Stampede. Everyone except him had quite a laugh. He finally escaped and ran as fast as he could away from that camel.

When the new millennium rolled around, we and many of our friends had a pretty good idea of where we wanted to be. If Y2K was going to do any damage at all worldwide, we wanted to be in the last place that it would touch on this planet—our desert campsite. We had quite a gathering that weekend, probably thirty or so people, all hanging out, laughing, and telling stories as we waited for any catastrophic events that might be coming about. Then again, we most likely would have been the last people in the world to know about it.

That evening, as the sun plummeted into the Sahara Desert, we looked like a bunch of rock hyraxes perched up on the rock outcroppings. In Botswana and South Africa, they have a term for these outcroppings, *kjoppies*, but I don't think there is an equivalent defining word in Arabic. The sight of the last sunset of the 1900s in Sudan was awe-inspiring for sure. God had painted a stunning picture of His creation that would be seared into many minds that night. No sooner had the sun melted into the sand than we had our campfire roaring and the food cooking. The evening was topped off by marshmallows and s'mores, along with some hot chocolate.

One interesting fact about deserts is that more people die from the cold at night than do from the heat in the daytime. Saddled by this knowledge, we wasted no time in getting our campfire blazing and kept it going most of the night. Mornings were often bitterly cold, and the first one up was responsible for reigniting the fire and brewing the coffee.

There was plenty of work that kept us busy in the country. By this time, I was working for an international sports development company. The level of sports in Sudan at that time was woeful at best. At one time, Sudanese athletes were right up there on the world scene, but with the tumultuous times in the country over the past decade or two, they had some serious need of revival. Our company was able to bring in some top caliber coaches, trainers, and teams to help jumpstart some of their aging programs. We saw particular success in raising the level of tennis and basketball. One of the coaches we brought in for the national basketball program was Coach Bob. He was about seventy-two years old, had a voice you could hear a kilometer away, and had as much energy as any twenty-year-old on the court. I vividly remember the first time I saw him running up and down the court with the national team and thinking, *Now that is the kind of shape I want to be in when I'm his age.* Well, now that I have reached that point, I have enjoyed the Master's graciousness to me. I think I might be very close to reaching that lofty goal. I just need my knees and ankles to miraculously not degenerate anymore—or have brand new bionic ones put in their place![4]

---

4. I actually now have one bionic knee and will soon be getting an ankle to match it!

Chapter 22

PROJECTS AND PROGRAMS

My kids certainly remember Coach Bob. Though of grandfatherly age, he was not all that *kid friendly*. Not that he was a grouch by any means; he just simply had a way about himself that he expected certain things out of others, children or not, and if you didn't meet up to his standards, with his megaphone voice he would let you know. He was also a deep well of stories. He had had quite some success, not only in America, but in other countries around the world, and in particular, China. He was one of the first American basketball coaches in China when it opened up to foreigners, and he got a first-hand look at some of the young talent that was there, including Yao Ming, who went on to have quite a career in the NBA. Though Coach Bob is now enjoying the immaculate courts in heaven, his legacy lives on in both the golf and basketball halls of fame in Illinois. I can vouch for the fact that he was universally loved in Sudanese basketball circles, and if you could find any of those youngsters from the nineties today, they could certainly tell you some Coach Bob stories.

We were also engaged in a variety of community building projects while there. One of the more successful ones was in one of the displaced camps on the far south side of the city. It was made up of mostly southerners who had fled the civil war. In the south the men were often conscripted right out of their homes to fight in the bloody conflict, so if they found an opportunity to flee to the city, even though it was in "enemy" territory, it was a much better option than dying in battle. This was also true of the western tribes who fled the war in Darfur. To be sure, it was not always smooth sailing living in Khartoum. Due to their history and the current war, tensions were often high, and little sparks could flare up easily.

We started a sewing project in that camp to help the women find gainful employment and some dignity. We began with six machines and trained the women for six weeks before sending them off with their own machines and the skills to sew garments that would clothe their families or their neighbors—or even school kids. We tried to choose women from different areas of the camp so as not to have too many machines in one area. We found an excellent woman to lead the project who already had some good sewing skills, and she wholeheartedly embraced the challenge of the project. It was so successful that after three years, she was running the center by herself, and the profits were able to supply her salary and meet the needs of the center.

At the same time, because we were Christians, we also held Bible study classes each day. They were not mandatory but were very well attended. So well in fact that the Bible studies grew faster than the sewing project. We were able to accommodate more women outside in the courtyard, where the studies were held, than inside with limited space. That led us to begin showing *The Jesus Film* in one of the meeting centers in the camp. We had small portable CD players with very small seven-inch screens on them, kind of like a large iPhone of today. I once witnessed more than fifty people crammed in around one of those screens, watching the story of Jesus. It was a pretty amazing sight to behold.

Another of our coaches was Mike H. He was a former coach at Nick Bollettieri's tennis academy in Florida, and he came out on numerous occasions to work with some of the young talent in the capital. We put on several camps over the years, and Mike was well loved in the Sudanese tennis world. The last year he came out, he worked with a young sixteen-year-old kid who had lots of raw talent but never amounted to much because he couldn't keep his head in the game and didn't know a lick of tactics. In two weeks, Mike changed all of that, and the young man ended up beating the six-years-running national champion in a tournament that was attended by the president of the country. During that match, my wife and I were sitting in the VIP section in the row behind the president. At one point my wife leaned over to me and whispered, "Don't you remember what happened in Egypt to President Sadat? Don't ever sit this close to a president again." I replied that we had no choice as they were our assigned seats.

Speaking of presidents and tennis. One day when I went to play at the local club, I was invited by a friend, who was a former champion, to join him in a doubles match. We would be playing against the former president of the country and his partner. I was politely instructed not to be too rough on the president. Hmm, I didn't exactly follow that protocol very well. When I saw how aggressively he was playing against us, much of my grace just floated away. We won the match, and the president was so very kind afterward as we sipped karkadeh in the clubhouse together.

During our last year in Khartoum, we brought out a basketball team from the States for about two weeks of games and training. We traveled all over the country with them on a bus supplied by the government. We had security guards and media people with us the whole time, and it was quite an event around the country. We often had a full page of the local papers dedicated to our tour. We never lost a game, even when they gathered the best players from around the country to make an all-star team to play us. It was a lot of fun and allowed us to travel in places that very few foreigners had been allowed to go to up till that time.

At the last game, held in the capital, and before a packed-out crowd with several dignitaries in attendance, we were able to present gifts to the minister of sports and a couple of other officials. At the center-court closing ceremony, we decided to give the minister a beautiful Bible that they brought out from the States. I knew it was going to be pushing the envelope, but we all had confirmation from the Holy Spirit that this was the right thing to do. We also gave Bibles to a few of the other officials as well. A few days later, a friend of mine in security told me that one of the officials didn't set his new Bible down for two days! Carried it everywhere he went. I sure hope he was just as diligent about reading it. I hold on to the verse in Isaiah 55 that says, "It is the same with my word. I send it out and it always produces fruit. It will accomplish all I want it to, and it will prosper everywhere I send it."

Chapter 23

MOVING SOUTH (2001)

It was not long after that when we were asked to open up the work in Southern Sudan. That would require a major move to Nairobi, Kenya, because of the civil war which was still raging. There was no way to get from the north to the south unless you were in the military. I know because we tried. Numerous times.

There were many benefits in moving to Kenya. The most important one as far as the work was concerned was access to Southern Sudan. Nairobi was the unofficial headquarters of every NGO, humanitarian, and religious group that was working in the south, though there were not very many at that time. The networking capabilities were deep and expansive. From the huge UN center located in Runda, to the never-ending religious organizations that were clustered within the city, there was seemingly no end to the possibilities for interconnectedness with like-minded partners.

Kenya was also a country of astounding natural beauty. From the heights of Kilimanjaro and Mount Kenya to the seashores of the Indian Ocean, and all the plains and deserts in between, it is a nature lover's paradise. Our family certainly tried to use every opportunity to go exploring as many of these attractions as we could. One year we went to the Masai Mara around the time of the great migration. Stayed in a tented camp, saw all kinds of wildlife, and enjoyed a great getaway for a few days. The unfortunate part of the Mara was getting to and from there. The one road was so bad that an entire private charter plane industry was created just to get tourists there and back.

But as we were residents and had our own vehicle, there was no need to spend the exorbitant amounts for flights when we could drive. And we were used to bad roads in Africa. Or so I thought. The road, which at one time was "paved," was at the worst end of terrible. It was a challenge to even find any remaining patches of the original paving in between the moon-crater expanses that dotted the road. When driving on these types of terrains it is important to give one hundred percent of your attention to the patch of land directly in front of you, and then make wise decisions about what your next move will be. These are often split-second decisions that can have undesirable consequences. Such was the case on our way back that day.

Trying to decide whether to avoid a large pothole or a small-sized boulder blocking the road, I made the wrong decision. The next thing we know, we are on our side in a trench beside the road, wedged in. Thankfully we were going fairly slow, and no one was injured. We had to crawl out through the doors that now faced the sky and flag down some help from passers-by. After sending April and Kate home with some kind strangers who happened along, Caleb and I stayed around until a tow truck, that someone had called for us, came and literally dragged us out of the trench. I think they actually did more damage to the vehicle while extracting it from the ditch than I did putting it in there! At any rate, Caleb and I were able to drive the vehicle home that evening and the next day took it to the mechanic to be repaired. Until this day, my family recalls that incident on a regular basis to poke fun at Dad's driving skills.

The pilots at AIM Air and MAF became some of our best friends. Their kids went to the same schools as ours, and their mission was very much in line with what we were looking at accomplishing among some of the poorest people on the planet. We spent a lot of time with them, both up in the air as well as on the ground. Some of my deepest strategic conversations were with them as they each had a very broad view of the different areas and tribes that existed in the south.

During the first few years of my time in Southern Sudan, one could barely find a scrap of paper laying on the ground. Everything was recyclable. In this facet, the Southern Sudanese were light-years ahead of the rest of the world. The big difference was *why* they were so green. It was not out of concern for the planet as a whole, as most of them did not know about any of the world's problems. There were no televisions, and there was no electricity, no running water, no source of news other than a rare shortwave radio or word of mouth. They simply reused everything out of necessity until it was in tatters. I still remember going to homes in the bush that were still using hand-carved wooden utensils. And the money we used during the early years was often sewn together or taped to keep it in one piece. I have some great remnants in my Southern Sudan collection.

In those early days we had to ship in virtually everything we desired for living, or we didn't have it. This included fuel, food, medicines and supplies for the clinic, toilet paper, spare parts for our vehicles, and any building supplies we always seemed to need. This took some meticulous planning as you had to predict just exactly how much you would be needing months in advance, purchase it well in advance, store it until you shipped it overland, arrange the transport from Kenya or Uganda, hope you didn't have to pay too many bribes on the way up, and pray that it didn't get hijacked by rebels somewhere on the trip north. Occasionally we would have an *oops* when ordering these supplies. One time the large *lorry* (truck) arrived at our compound with bales and bales of toilet paper. We had enough to last us about twenty-five years. We were giving it away as presents. What had happened was Kate read/interpreted that a bundle of toilet paper was ten rolls when in actuality it was ten bundles of ten rolls. She had planned on one hundred rolls, and we got one thousand. We were building toilet paper castles in our spare time! Among other things, it certainly increased our spare time creativity.

Chapter 24

PRAYER AS PRIORITY

Though this chapter should certainly be earlier in this book, I need to mention the significant and crucial role of a prayer team in the lives of people living on the field overseas. I can attest to the fact that without our War Room of steady and faithful pray-ers over the years (called the Warriors), we would certainly not have been overseas as long as we have. In the early days, before the internet changed the way business is done, our prayer updates back home were our lifeline. They continued to be so until we left the field in 2022, but they changed in their form of execution. Back in the eighties there was no *instant gratification* or *immediate answer to our supplications,* as workers of today can often attest to. The workers reaching the field today can send out tweets or texts and know that they have people praying for them instantly and *in the moment* as they are in the midst of work or a crisis nine thousand miles away. They can even send updates telling all of their supporters how God answered their pleas. For us, in those early days, we would sometimes send out a request one month and not remember to tell our supporters back home how God had answered that request until about three months later when we sent out our next requests. We *did* send out an end-of-the-year update reminding our Warriors of all that God had answered over the course of the preceding year. It is amazing that almost all of them have stuck with us over the years and through the countries. Did this change the way God was working? I don't think so. At the same time, thinking about some of the things our family went through without anyone knowing except the Master himself, makes me wonder about the direction of our faith.

One wonderful prayer story that comes to my mind was during the time that we were doing medical clinics north of Rumbek with Ann and Bala Rao's teams. We had a couple of vehicles loaded with medical personnel as well as two Bible storytellers. One of those storytellers was a pastor from Dallas by the name of Tim Ahlen. This is the story Tim told about their time in a village called Aliet. I witnessed this, but it is Tim's story.

> *Aliet was the most remote of the villages we visited. It is located about four miles north of Ma'en. The road to the village is little more than a bicycle path. We went there on Friday morning because one of the residents had come to Ma'en and told us that the people of the village needed to hear the Word of God. When we arrived, we were greeted by a small number of village leaders, including one of the sub-chiefs. We sat down and began to talk to a group of about twenty-five children and adults. We immediately sensed an attitude of opposition. The sub-chief informed us that there was already a church in the village and they did not need another one.*

After further conversation, it became clear that the village only had services on Christmas day, and that the people were unaware of what it meant to be a follower of Christ. We told a few stories. Then as we finished for the day, we were reminded that there was a serious epidemic of meningitis, a lot of dysentery, some malaria, and other illnesses in the village. We visited one tukul, in which there was a small boy who was very sick with meningitis, and his older brother, who was suffering with dysentery. We prayed intensely for both the boys and left for Ma'en, unsure if the boy with meningitis would survive as he was in very bad shape. We went back later and administered the only dose of medication we had and gave the older boy some medication for his dysentery.

The next day we stopped by the village again, on our way back from Amook. The boy with meningitis, who could not lift himself up the day before, was out playing football with his friends. We promised the people we would return on Tuesday to teach them the Word of God, and then left. When we returned to Aliet on Tuesday, there was quite a difference in the attitudes and receptivity of the people. About 110 people gathered around us to hear our Bible stories. After we were done, more prayer and healing happened. One little boy was limp in his parents' arms when they laid him at our feet. We laid hands on him and prayed in Jesus' name. The boy sat up by himself! The next day we found out that he was all better. We finished our time with a prayer for the whole community and declared that God was now the Lord of Aliet.

NOT QUITE FINISHED

This was just an abbreviated story of what we often saw when prayer was offered up to the Healer of all who come to Him.

Chapter 25

GOD'S INTERVENTION

While still located in Kenya that first year, I got a call from some young men who were studying at the local Baptist seminary up in Brackenhurst. They were Sudanese young men who were about to graduate in a week or two, and they had heard that I was working in the south. When I met them a couple of weeks later, they put a proposal, or should I say request, before me, asking if I would help them to get back into Southern Sudan. They announced that they had now been trained and were ready to change the face of church planting in the south. Two were Dinka, and two were Nuer. Wonderful young men, but I was very leery of bringing them into the work we had already started because it didn't fit in with the methodology of church planting that was being taught in the seminary at that time. I told them as much.

That first meeting certainly didn't go as they had planned or hoped, but being the eternal optimists that most Sudanese are, they didn't give up. I remember we had two or three more meetings where they pleaded with me to give them a try. In the end, we wrote up an agreement where I stipulated some pretty stringent requirements that they would need to follow if we were to work together. Without thinking too very much about those requirements, they all readily agreed to what I laid out. I think they thought that once they got back to the south, they would be the ones who were the *knowers*, and I would be the outsider White guy. What they didn't take into account was the amount of time they had all been outside of their home country. Each one had been out for between eight and fourteen years, and during that time of war and fighting and hunger, the land they knew as kids or very young men was not the same as the one they were returning to.

My first requirement was that they all come to the village of Akot initially, though none of them were from that area. I wanted them to be living in the homes of some of the leaders that we had been working with over the past couple of years. We had been training these leaders in the Bible storying method, and that was something that none of the new guys knew about. They were to stay with our leaders for three to four months of training, and at the end of that time, I would send them each back to their home areas where they could start their own work.

I recall the day the plane arrived on that very same airstrip I had first come in on, and off stepped three of those young men (the fourth came a bit later). The first one off, who we would soon give the nickname "the governor," hopped out of that little Cessna in a three-piece suit and wingtip shoes! That image is stamped in my memory for eternity. That plane was surrounded by people who owned one pair of clothes, maybe a pair of flip-flops, a spear, and a bunch of cattle. They must have thought that he actually was the governor. Oh, and did I mention it was about one hundred and ten degrees on that dirt runway?

I knew then and there that I would have a real challenge with him, but much to his credit, after those initial months of struggle he had some very kind words to say about the rigors of what they had gone through. They had all forgotten how to take a "shower" with a small bucket of water hauled from a not-so-nearby well, how to relieve themselves in the bush and not in a bathroom with a toilet, how to walk or ride a bike for great distances instead of taking a matatu, how precious water was since there were no taps with running water anywhere, how different and scarce food was because there was no place to actually buy any from a shop, or how hot it was without any fans to cool them or electricity at night to read by. All of those things that they had gotten used to while in Kenya were gone, and their memories were scrambling.

It wasn't always so easy for them as when they were at seminary. They had all met up in the refugee camp in Kakuma, just along the northern border of Kenya. Some of them came into their relationship with Jesus in that camp. One of them had been on the *long march* from up along the Ethiopian border all the way to Kakuma.

Chapter 26

THE LONG MARCH

During the second Sudanese Civil War (1987–2005), children were unable to adequately support themselves and suffered greatly from the terror. Many children were orphaned or separated from their families because of the systematic attacks of genocide in the southern part of the country. Some children were able to avoid capture or death because they were away from their villages, tending cattle at the cattle camps (grazing land located near bodies of water where cattle were taken and tended largely by the village children during the dry season), and were able to flee and hide in the dense African bush. Some of the unaccompanied male minors were conscripted by the Islamic southern rebel terrorist forces and used as soldiers in the rebel army, while others were handed over to the Islamic State by their own families to ensure protection and food and under a false impression the child would be attending school. Children were highly marginalized during this period. As a result, they began to conglomerate in an effort to flee the country and the war.

Motivated by the loss of their parents and their need to find food and safety from the conflict, an estimated twenty thousand boys from rural Southern Sudan fled to bordering Ethiopia and Kenya. Much of the travel took place by foot in large groups, with the boys traveling in single-file lines. The journey from Southern Sudan to the nearest refugee camp could be thousands of miles. Travel ranged from a span of weeks to two or more years. Often the children traveled with no possessions besides the clothes on their backs. The boys often depended on the charity of villages they passed for food, necessities, and treatment of the sick. However, most of their travel was in isolated regions with very little infrastructure. Groups of boys were often organized and led by the oldest boy in the group, who could be a young adult or sometimes as young as ten or twelve years old.

They were vulnerable to heat exhaustion, pneumonia, malaria, and other diseases for which they had little means of prevention or treatment. Additionally, attacks by lions, snakes, and other wild animals were not uncommon. It is estimated that over half of the young migrants died along their journey due to starvation, dehydration, disease, attacks by wild animals, and enemy soldiers. Conditions were made even more dangerous by the SPLA soldiers (Sudanese Peoples Liberation Army), who would attack the boys or forcibly recruit them as child soldiers. The SPLA estimated that twelve hundred boys were recruited from groups of displaced children, although they deny forcing any of them into conflict. Experts say the Lost Boys are the most badly war-traumatized children ever examined.

The journey of the Lost Boys was filled with suffering and unknowns as the boys rarely knew the direction they were headed. Initially, most of the fleeing boys went to a refugee camp in Ethiopia, until the war in 1991 sent the boys fleeing again to a different refugee camp called Kakuma, which is located in Northern Kenya. The arrival of the Lost Boys to the refugee camps in Ethiopia and Kenya was welcomed to various degrees. It was difficult for the camps to provide sufficient food for the hundreds of boys arriving daily. The Lost Boys came to the camps without guardians or adult supervision. They immediately required housing and schooling, which changed the allocation of resources in the camps. With some of the boys arriving in the camps at ages as young as six or seven, many of the Boys spent the majority of their childhood and adolescence being raised in the camps. Ultimately, being raised in a refugee camp significantly altered their development and ability to assimilate into regular life.[5]

I heard many stories from them, and others, over the years, but there is one that is very special to me. It came from Ding, one of the Nuer. After a few years in Kakuma, he had risen to the position of a pastor of one of the churches in the camp. One day, as he was up front preaching, he saw a man come in through the door in the back of the church. Ding immediately recognized him as the man who had killed his uncle in a tribal dispute. These disputes can go back generations between the two tribes. Others inside the church also recognized the man and expected Ding to extract his family's revenge for the killing. Most of his family members walked out of the church. Yet Ding, now being filled with the Holy Spirit, took a different tactic. He forgave him. The man walked out of the church in fear prior to the service ending. Ding's family members found him and told the man what Ding told them—that there was no other way for the tribes of Southern Sudan to move forward without forgiveness. He had learned this from the teachings of Jesus in the scriptures. What a great example Ding was that day to the people in his church. Even though his family members all encouraged him

---
5. Wikipedia

to seek revenge, he refused. Eventually each of them came around to Ding's biblical approach and forgave the man. And I can honestly say that in the years I have known him, he has always exemplified that very same heart.

One year while Ding was visiting in Nairobi, we invited him over to our house for Christmas dinner. We had purchased a USB thumb drive for him as a small gift. When he saw it, he was so excited. He said that that was his first-ever Christmas gift from someone. That Sudanese mile-wide smile of pearly whites shone brightly that day.

Chapter 27

STARTING OUT IN THE SOUTH

When initially moving to the south, we looked at the enormity of the task before us and realized we would need some help. Because we began by operating a small medical clinic in Akot, which we took over from Samaritan's Purse, we saw that we could bring in medical teams to help with programs at the clinic, as well as create bush clinics to reach out to the multitudes who could not make the trek in. In those early years when we would return to the States, we began connecting with some key churches and eventually were able to create a coalition with three of them to work alongside of us in a variety of programs.

Southern Sudan was a literal hotbed of disease. This led us to our initial focus on this crucial area of improvement for the Dinka in our area. The diseases there ranged from malaria, which took more lives than any other disease, to Ebola, which was also a terrifying disease. We saw cases of nodding syndrome, a form of epilepsy that was devastating to young children; diarrhea, which was fairly common; Guinea worm disease, which, thanks to Jimmy's Carter's organization (The Carter Center), was nearly eradicated during our time there, with the new date for global eradication of 2024; sleeping sickness (African trypanosomiasis), which reared its head after years of downward cases; river blindness, which was everywhere (onchocerciasis); and elephantiasis, which can make one's legs look like an elephant. Leprosy, tuberculosis, and Buruli ulcers were everywhere as well, and the cures for these maladies were in very short supply.

One of the scariest diseases in the world, AIDS, was almost non-existent while we were there, simply because there was a civil war going on and very few trucks made their way across our borders. It was the truck drivers who were spreading it all across Africa. In other neighboring countries like Uganda, where 1.5 million people are infected by HIV, about 400,000 people have died from the disease.

All of these and so many more diseases flourished in a land that had constant flooding and droughts, not to mention a lack of doctors. When we lived there, I believe there were less than twenty doctors in the country, which at that time had a population of about eight million people. There were very few fully functioning hospitals as well. Many were simply buildings where people came to die because of the lack of medicines and vaccines.

A lot of what we did initially was due to these medical conditions in Southern Sudan. We could see that the absolute scarcity of sustainable hospitals, and the great need for medicines and supplies, would be an area where we could assist the people in a physical way. The difference was that we were bringing Jesus along with our service to the people.

Chapter 28

MEDICAL ASSISTANCE

At this point our medical work took off, with much thanks to Dawson Avenue Baptist Church and Idlewild Baptist Church, who both had strong teams of experienced medical personnel. We were joined later by Bill Deans and Mustard Seed International, who eventually built a brand-new hospital just down the road from the clinic. Unfortunately, that hospital is in a very run-down state now and not serving the Akot district today like it was twenty years ago.

There were some very key individuals who made many, many trips out to work with us. One of the first was Debbie Moss from Dawson. She was a kind of pioneer for us and helped us "break ground" in the bush clinic operations. Then Ann and Bala Rao from Idlewild came along shortly after and got the ball rolling even faster. And in the midst of these groups came Jeff Deal, an ENT surgeon from East Cooper Baptist Church, who provided much-needed wisdom and vision in the medical sphere as we made plans to ramp up that phase of the work. Our relationship with Jeff and his family became a strong bond over the years, and Jeff even wrote an excellent book about the Dinka people called *The Mark*.[6] His insights were always a valuable addition to any discussion we had, whether it was in the medical realm, on social ministries, or with church-related activities and practices. We didn't always agree on everything, but his wisdom was always the kind that made me think deeper about any decisions I would be making. Over the years, all of Jeff's family, at one time or another, walked the paths of Akot, serving the King in any way they could. His four kids, plus his wife, Hart, all made major contributions in helping the Dinka to a higher standard of life and a deeper walk with God during their days with us.

The third partner in the coalition was from Shady Grove Baptist Church. The minister of music there, Rob Miller, was a friend of Kate and mine from our early days at Sheridan Hills, and Rob actually sang in our wedding. Pat Cronin was the pastor at that time and was also a colleague from Sheridan Hills. He and Rob spearheaded their involvement with Dawson and Idlewild and made many trips to Akot. One of their first projects was helping us to construct a structure for our oral Bible school. It also served as an office and library for the local leaders. We used two shipping containers, with a roof connecting the two of them and a slab underneath the roof, giving much-needed shade and space to have classes. I'm confident that it is one of the strongest structures ever built in the south and will be there long after I go to my grave.

---

6. Jeff Deal, *The Mark* (Scotts Valley, CA: CreateSpace Independent Publishing Platform, December 4, 2013).

Chapter 29

CATTLE CAMPS

One of the projects we did in our area was cattle camp storying. Storying is a form of presenting the Bible, and God's heart for His people, in the form of stories—which is the way many people around the world best understand the scriptures. The cattle camps in Southern Sudan are legendary. They are some of the toughest mini-environments of any place I know. Tougher than being in the slums of Kabira in Nairobi or on the south side of Chicago. A lot of articles have been written about them in detail and are fascinating reading. One *National Geographic* book was done by Carol Beckwith, along with photographs by Angela Fisher, called *The Dinka: Legendary Cattle Keepers of Sudan*.[7] Another one was a *Time-Life* compilation done by John Ryle and Sarah Errington called *Warriors of the White Nile*.[8] These books and

---

7. Carol Beckwith and Angela Fisher, *The Dinka* (NY: Rizzoli, 2010).

8. John Ryle and Sarah Errington, *Warriors of the White Nile: The Dinka (Peoples of the Wild)* (Amsterdam: Time Life Books, January

articles will give one an in-depth look at the harshness of these micro-communities within the Dinka and other tribes in the south.

I clearly remember my first visit to one of these camps. I had been harshly told that I could not go into one without the accompaniment of a local Dinka man who had ties with that particular camp. That opportunity came when I finally went in with a couple of our church leaders and was welcomed with smiles and greetings that were clearly not-so-hidden suspiciousness. *Why was this White man coming into our domain? What did he want? What was he looking for? Why does he want to take pictures and walk around our camp?* All of these and more were questions that we were met by in those first tense moments in camp. I would venture that only a handful of White faces have ever entered into these camps over the centuries. Suspicions were high. Foreigners were not generally welcome. After all, there was a civil war raging at that time.

Oh, and did I mention that cattle rustling was certainly a thing in Southern Sudan? Which reminds me of the time Kate and I were driving along the road to Akot one day when we saw a group of mean-looking young men herding cattle across the road we were on. As we approached, suddenly the AK-47s came up and pointed in our direction. I slowed but didn't stop until a bullet went whizzing past our vehicle. At that point, reverse seemed like the wise decision to make. It was then that we realized they were not just herding the cattle but rustling them.

One of the first things to hit you in the camps is the number of flies. Everywhere. There is a reason that they keep smoky ashen fires going all the time. Not only flies, but malaria and dengue-fever-carrying mosquitos are rampant. Prior to some mass distribution efforts to give mosquito nets

---

1, 1982).

CATTLE CAMPS

to a majority of the population, there was constant sickness in these camps. There still is, but at least malaria and dengue fever have seen a great decrease for those that use the nets. As mentioned earlier, there are still a dozen other diseases that are either eradicated or unknown in other parts of the world that can kill. Just part of life in the camps. And AIDS had yet to come in any significant way to Southern Sudan.

The fires and ash serve not only the Dinka but their beloved cattle as well. Keeping the constant disease-carrying pests away from their living "banks"—their cattle—is paramount in the camps. From my perspective, the flies didn't seem to mind the smoke all that much and were a constant irritant while inside that environment. Knowing the number of diseases they can also carry and transmit was very troubling.

One of the next things I noticed was the number of guns. AKs everywhere. Even a few old, almost ancient rifles from wars past. Where they got the ammo for those relics, I'll never know. There were a lot of spears as well, but somehow next to the AKs they didn't seem so foreboding. On occasion there would be an old Dinka shield lying around. During my years in the south, I saw very few of those relics of their grandparents' generation. I was actually able to purchase one from a Dinka, as well as one from the Nuer tribe, who live a bit further north and are the Dinka's nemesis. Though I was offered AKs to purchase on several different occasions while in the south, I knew that getting one out of that country, into another African country, and all the way into the States would be something that probably would never happen. And not purchasing one would surely keep me out of a prison somewhere.

We took several months talking over and planning the project to put storytelling evangelists in those camps. One of our first hurdles was finding believers willing to leave their family for months at a time to go into that environment.

Most of our believers didn't want anything to do with that flash from their past. They knew how very rough and tumble those camps could be. And selling their presence in those camps for weeks at a time would be a real challenge. As we were looking at the future and how to send out the gospel to the far reaches of South Sudan, we saw that the cattle camps, which were constantly on the move for pastureland, would be a perfect vehicle. Finally, a couple of young men, not yet married, volunteered for the assignment.

Though it was really rough for them, they persevered over a season and did a great job of storying the gospel and many other stories to the camps they entered. It was not long after that that Kate and I left that area and, as far as we know, no follow-up has been done to see if our expected and hopeful results of transmission were successful. One day I hope to return to that area and enquire from the leaders if that dream of churches being planted in cattle camps came to fruition.

Chapter 30

OUTREACH

Another project we had was sending young committed workers, who were trained in storying the Bible, into some of the more remote areas of the south. One of the places where we started work was about four to five hours east, up the river from Malakal. There was a small landing strip there that could be used in the dry season. But in the rainy season, its black cotton soil made it impossible for anything to land or take off. It was then that we would fly into Malakal and take a boat up the river.

The work started there through the medical camps we were doing. As one of our original young men from the Kenyan seminary, John Monychol, was from that village, Abwong, we took medical teams up there a few times. It was on the south side of the river, which was the demarcation line of the north and the south. My first time flying in there, I disembarked from our Cessna Caravan and was promptly greeted by a young soldier with a fifty-caliber machine gun strapped to his back and bandoliers of ammo hanging off of his shoulders. It was then that I realized how close we were to the front lines of the war. As we walked into the village, I noticed numerous very deep craters scattered everywhere and was informed that these were the remnants of the mortar attacks from the other side of the river.

One of the young men that John was training was working with some of the many soldiers who were stationed in that area. While I was up there one day, he complained to me of all the work he was doing, only to have the soldiers be sent to another area of the war zones. He said each time he began to get a group of believers together, their commander would send them off to another area. I helped him look at this from another perspective. Rather than feeling depressed that all the work he was doing was amounting to nothing in his village, I helped him see that he was, in fact, training these men up to be evangelists that are "sent out" and that they could be starting their own groups wherever they were sent. Little did I imagine that this very scenario would be a complaint of mine twenty years later as I watched one after another trained disciple leave our country to go to other places. So very often we lose sight of God's much bigger picture and zero in on the work we have planted, worked, and nurtured. So, as I have now watched several young men that I have worked with grow and mature into proclaimers of the Word, I have been able to find a peace about *letting them go* and trusting the Master's bigger plan.

I am most happy to report that John is still serving the King in his region of South Sudan. He is now working with a dear friend of mine, Mike Congrove. Mike is the executive director and co-founder of Empower One. They have planted themselves in South Sudan and are doing some amazing Kingdom work there. He got a great leader when he hired John to work alongside of them.

Chapter 31

WARRIORS THROUGH AND THROUGH

One odd thing about the Dinka, and something that is surely attributable to their upbringing, was made readily known to me during my first year working in Akot. As Nurse Wycliffe and I were sitting in our compound one afternoon, talking to one of the young men from that area, there came some very loud *boom-booms* from the village (which was two kilometers away). The sounds of gunfire continued to amplify for some time when all of a sudden Wycliffe and I see this mass of Dinka men making their way through the bush toward the sounds of war—most of them carrying a weapon of some sort. During that same time, Wycliffe and I are thinking through and making plans to evacuate should those sounds get louder and closer. The two of us just looked at each other and commented, "What kind of people run *toward* fighting instead of away from it?" What we had to take into consideration was that up to that point in time, every Dinka person alive who was under the age of twenty-five had lived his entire life waking up every single day wondering, *Will I have to flee my home today? Who in my family will be killed today? Will all of our crops get looted by marauding soldiers or militias? Will I be conscripted into fighting for the army today?*, or any number of other questions that are the inevitability of an ongoing civil war. In this case, the second of two twenty-year wars. This was an important piece of the understanding that was needed to relay the gospel to these people. It had a bearing on the stories we told from the Bible.

Yet another issue related to these civil wars was the fact that an entire segment of the population was almost non-existent. The population of men between the ages of twenty-five and fifty had almost vanished due to the war. That left a huge hole in the generational upbringing of the young people. While there, we often witnessed a glaring gap between the youth and the over-fifty-year-old leaders. Not having that crucial "go-between" generation that could pass down important traditions and cultural intricacies often made decision making a challenging process. The youth didn't want to listen to the *old people,* and the wiser leaders felt they were not being respected by the hot-headed youth. I was able to sit around many community circles where decisions were hashed out and witnessed the uneasiness and distrust between the two generations.

Chapter 32

KINGDOM HEARTS

Back to Ann and Bala. They, and their Sunday school class's involvement in Akot over a ten-plus-year span, was nothing short of amazing. Beginning with medical work teams and participating in some building projects, well drilling, evangelistic crusades, church planting, to building and running schools and women's training programs, they had a key hand in improving Dinka life in Akot. They, along with Jeff and the others, will long be remembered for their sacrificial love for the people. Ann later started her own organization (Living Water Community Transformation, livingwaterct.org) through which she and Bala almost single-handedly plowed on when many of us had left the area. Their organization is currently heavily involved in working with refugees and displaced Sudanese from the current fighting taking place in the south. They are doing some incredible Kingdom work in Northern Uganda, even as I write this.

Kate and I owe a huge debt to everyone who came to one of the most isolated and overlooked places on the planet.

Working alongside a people who were living far in the past when we initially encountered them—without running water, without readily available medical assistance, constant food shortages, and little to no educational opportunities—was both a challenge and a blessing. The Kingdom hearts of so many people who worked hand-in-hand with us, and often exceeded what we had envisioned, was truly a remarkable time of unity for us.

The physical part of life was a continual challenge in the south. When things broke, you fixed them. When you didn't have the right part for a repair, you improvised and made something work. Often you would repair a particular item over and over again, like our solar power system, our water system, our vehicle, and most anything that had moving parts. I can't count the number of times when I had to repair a broken-down vehicle out in the middle of the bush with little more than a handful of basic tools. Having a full-suite multi-tool and a roll of duct tape was not optional; it was essential.

We were in a constant battle with the elements and nature itself. We had a five-year running war with bats and mice in our roof (we won a battle or two but definitely lost that war). Scorpions, snakes, and other stinging creatures were a constant. Gratefully we never did get bitten by any of the multitude of very poisonous snakes that slithered through our property. We probably killed about one a month on average. The scorpions and other painful stingers did a much better job at inflicting pain on us. One time, when I stuck my hand in the laundry basket to take out the clothes to be washed, I got a nasty sting on one of my fingers. I quickly took what measures I thought were prudent and seemed to have kept the pain localized and to a minimum. That is until my wonderful wife came over to me and said, "I know what will take the pain away. Just put your finger in this bowl." The bowl was half full of vinegar, and not knowing much about scorpion pain relief tactics, I did as I was told. Within about ten seconds, I let out a torturous screech that had our compound guard come running up to our door, inquiring about my safety. It was only a short while later when my wife admitted that maybe that cure was for a *different* critter's bite that she had read about. A couple of months later she got stung by a scorpion in the sink, and I informed her that I knew just the cure for her pain! She chose other methods.

One of my and my daughter's greatest joys and memories of Southern Sudan was being able to baptize April in the Bahr Naam River. On one of Jeff Deal's many trips to Akot, he had a couple of his kids with him, and they asked to be baptized while they were there. My daughter was also in-country at that time, and she, too, wanted to be baptized. So we made arrangements with some of the local church leaders, piled in as many people as possible into our vehicles, and drove down to a section of the road that goes between Akot and Rumbek where a bridge crosses the river. Because it was the time of year when the water flow was manageable, we found a small area that was somewhat off to the side of the main flow and was shallow enough for us to walk out in. It was there that I was blessed to be able to baptize April, and Jeff's daughters were baptized by one of our local pastors. April remembers putting on two pairs of knee-high socks to stand in the muddy water in hopes of warding off any parasites that might have wanted to make their new home in her. Since I only had shorts on, I'm sure they would have chosen me as their new residence.

Another joy for me was having my kids come into Southern Sudan with me. I don't recall them ever coming in together, mostly due to separate school schedules. But the time I got to spend with them individually was always very rich and rewarding. Something about being in a little Cessna puddle-jumper plane, skirting through clouds, which was not Caleb's favorite thing to do, or scampering through the bush on a motorcycle or four-wheeler, which *was* his favorite thing to do, makes memories that are hard to forget. Being able to walk side-by-side, experiencing the hardships and challenges of a people considered to be "the least of these," creates a bond that is hard to replace. Walking into a clinic where people were dying from malaria, snakebites, or gunshot wounds has a lasting impression in one's mind—especially a young mind. I'm quite sure that those experiences helped to shape a culture of compassion in both of my children.

One of those trips really sticks out in April's mind. It was her first trip in with just me. She had gotten out of school ten days early during her junior year at Rift Valley Academy due to bomb threats at the school. With those extra "free days," that was the perfect time for her introduction to South Sudan 101. Though we both remember that the tiny no-see-um bugs did quite a nasty number on her legs, she has vivid memories of sitting out at night in our bamboo lawn chairs, looking up at a sky that was chock full of stars and planets, and just talking the night away with me. She remembers asking me all sorts of questions that she had never asked before, like when and how Kate and I met, what it was like growing up in my family, and some other intimate things about my life. A very special memory for her and for me.

Traveling to and from Southern Sudan was rarely effortless, especially in the early days when there were no scheduled flights and no airlines flying in and out of the country. After five or six years, some airlines out of Kenya started scheduled flights to a couple or three towns in the south. There were often glitches—planes late or not coming at all, limited luggage space, detours once in the air, etc. There was one time when Kate and I had meetings to attend in Uganda. This meant that we had to travel through Juba on our way to Kampala. Kate traveled a day or two ahead of me, as her meeting started earlier than mine. She had traveled from Rumbek to Juba on a UN flight that only required her to show her NGO ID, so she didn't look at the passport until after she checked in for the commercial flight in Juba and was stamped out of Southern Sudan by immigration officials. As she was looking through the passport, she realized she had *my* passport instead of hers. For the officials in Juba, that didn't seem to be an issue as she breezed through immigration without any issues. But when she reached Uganda, she realized there was a problem, even though the immigration officials there didn't seem to notice or care. Apparently neither the airline nor the immigration officials had realized it was the wrong passport. The Ugandan immigration official was about to stamp the passport to allow her entry into Uganda when she stopped him with, "But this is not my passport; I have my husband's passport by mistake. He will come in two days with my passport, and we can switch."

"No problem," replied the official. "Leave his passport here, and when he arrives, come back, and we will stamp you both in on your own passports."

When I arrived in Juba two days later, the immigration officers didn't think too kindly about me traveling on my wife's passport. I'm quite sure that in most countries around the world that would have been the end of my journey right then and there. But I explained what had happened and managed to sweet-talk the officials, in Arabic, to allow me to continue on. Once I arrived in Kampala, Kate was at the airport, where she had surrendered my passport to the officials there, and where we finally sorted everything out and were officially allowed to enter their country.

In 2004 we recruited two young men, both from Florida, to come and help us proclaim the gospel into some far-reaching areas where others had not gone. James and Ryan were terrific guys who were as different as lions and elephants but worked together wonderfully because of those differences. One special quality we remember about James was his willingness to do whatever was needed to accomplish a task. One of their key assignments was to ride bikes all over the district as they told biblical stories to whomever would listen. At one point, after building them a mud hut, we relocated them up to a village about one hundred kilometers (four hours by vehicle) north of Rumbek. Literally, to just about where the earth ends. As they were on bikes, it took them about twelve hours (I think). These were not ordinary bikes; rather, we had them specially ordered from a company in the States, and the boys brought them out with them. The *special* part here is that James didn't know how to ride a bike before taking this assignment. By the time he reached us, he had mastered the art, and by the time he and Ryan left the field, they were both sculpted young men with about two percent body fat at the most. It should be noted that this was way out of James' wheelhouse, as he was an English/fine arts major in college. Ryan, on the other hand, loved it out in the bush. Currently Ryan is leading a church up north in America, and James is on a team reaching unreached peoples overseas.

Another special memory that our whole family has is of the Sudan Six. In 2007 we had put in a request for two more young men to come and join us in the work, as it had expanded way beyond what we were capable of handling. The request got lots of interest, despite our writing it up as a terrible and difficult place to come and serve. Shortly after we got word that two guys had been selected to join us, we got another email telling us about two young ladies who wanted to come as well, and would we be willing to take them, too. *Sure, why not?* we thought. Then a third message came our way, telling us about two more young ladies who were answering a different job request and were begging to be part of the team. *OK, Lord, sounds like you have something planned way beyond what we have, so let's run with it.*

It turned out that this group of journeymen was absolutely amazing. They were all at the recruitment conference together where they met and started the bonding process. From there they went to many weeks of training together, where they worked out many of the team intricacies that often take place on the field. By the time they reached us in the bush, they had a very good jump-start on being a well-developed team. Very early on, five of them knew that one of the young men was not going to make it (as much as we tried to see that he did), and they were correct. He left after a few short weeks, which meant we were unbalanced.

God already had in the wings a young man, Jermaine, who quickly joined the team and re-balanced it out. One funny story about Jermaine (and there are many) was, prior to his arrival, all the young ladies were speculating on what he would look like—tall, blond hair, handsome, muscular, etc. When he arrived, he was about an inch shorter than all of them and weighed about 125 pounds dripping wet. Kate and I had one of our biggest laughs when we originally met him, prior to the team laying eyes on him. All said and done, Jermaine was a total delight and fit perfectly into the team—as if God didn't already know that would happen.

Jermaine loved the people there and even lived in a mud hut for many months in Akot at one point. It was while he was living down there that a team of youth came in from the Fusion program out of Midwestern Seminary to spend a month or so working alongside us at a number of locations in our district. One day several of them took a trip a few hours into the bush to a fishing village to tell stories from the Bible. The unfortunate part was that one of the young ladies, who was the daughter of a colleague of ours living in Uganda, went on that excursion without her EpiPen. She had severe allergies to bees, which were everywhere in Southern Sudan. And yes, she got stung and soon went into anaphylaxis. Well, young Jermaine assessed the situation quickly, turned that Land Cruiser in the direction of the hospital in Akot, and literally flew over those bush tracks. I'm quite sure no vehicle has ever made that trip in the time that they did. They called ahead on the radio, so the doctor was waiting with the EpiPen when they arrived. She survived.

The sad part of this story is that Kate and I didn't have any knowledge of this happening until one of our Sudan Six let it slip out in a conversation a few days later. Needless to say, there were some not very pleased team leaders at that point. Upon making a quick trip down to Akot to talk with the doctor first, and the team as a whole later, there were some new and very strict guidelines for staying where they were. The doctor informed me that the young lady had about thirty minutes of life left by the time she reached the hospital. I poured praise all over Jermaine for saving her life, while at the same time reminding him that he should have been in communication with us as this was going on. Good lessons learned for everyone. God's mercy flowed abundantly.

The other young man who paired up with Jermaine was Andres. Smart, laid back, level-headed, and always willing to do whatever it took to get a task done. Only once did his calmness come into question. He had been with us for about a year and a half, and we decided to allow him to tag along with Billy White (ex-Ranger in his seventies, found Jesus late in life, and worked with literacy programs with the SPLA) on a trip up to the north/south border, near to Darfur. Andres was going to do some research for us in that area to assess the church development programs going on. They were gone for a couple of successful weeks and were almost back to Rumbek when it happened. About ten kilometers outside of town, there was an ambush set up that had a tree or log blocking the road. It was about 10 p.m. (which violated our nighttime travel restrictions) when they came up to it, and Andres was driving because Billy was tired from driving most of that day. As Andres alerted Billy to the issue, Billy quickly told him to drive around it, which meant going into the ditch-like channel that parallels the gravel roads there. About that time, the AKs opened fire and thankfully only one window got blown out and no one was hit.

The next day, I spent a couple of hours debriefing Andres on his trip, and all sounded good. As we were walking back to his room at the compound they lived in, I noticed a little one-inch cut on his arm and asked him about it. "Oh, that was from when we ran through the ambush last night," came the reply. A very stunned team leader then had a *second* debriefing about the trip. Like I said, laid-back, calm, level-headed. . . .

A day later, when I went down to Akot to see the vehicle and hear Billy's rendition of the story (same as Andres'), I found a couple of bullets lodged into the vehicle's interior above the rearview mirror, along with the blown-out right rear window. I was sure glad that angels traveled along with our personnel.

I'm sure I could write about twenty pages worth of stories about the Sudan Six. They never ceased to amaze us. There was no project or program they weren't willing to tackle. The ones that they did lead were groundbreaking and long-lasting. Two of the young ladies, Whitney and Jennifer, wrote up a training program for AIDS awareness that combined local Dinka cultural stories alongside of pertinent biblical stories. It was so good that the UN started using it for their training modules. This program was produced to get ahead of the coming disease that had not yet overcome this country, unlike other sub-Saharan countries. The name of the program was, "The Disease That Has No Cure."

The other two young ladies, Laura and Jamie, with some help from our medical partners, designed a reusable sanitary napkin made from locally available materials. Then they taught the girls how to make them. That allowed a very large segment of school-aged girls to not miss a week of classes every month. It was a huge success in the community. They also taught English and other subjects to the women in that community as well as in Akot. About twenty minutes to the west of Rumbek was a leper colony, where the girls spent time telling Bible stories. They made a lot of friends in that community, which was shunned by most of the rest of the people.

One very special blessing during the dry season was the African sky at night. When you are located in a place that has zero residual light from anywhere for hundreds of miles around, it can be an awe-inspiring experience. It would be so dark inside our house that sometimes Kate and I would not be able to see each other when we were laying right next to one another on our bed. But once you were outside, with the canopy of light from the stars, it was a sight like no other. Though I have never had the privilege of going into space, I can certainly appreciate its vastness from the multitude of nights that I closed my weary eyes after gazing upon the Bear, the Big Dipper, Orion's Belt, and many other constellations, which were crystal-clear, and slept outside under God's special array of stellar light. Most of those nights were with our local bush dog, Fuata, lying beside us to warn us of any unsavory slithering critters coming our way. Sleeping outside was only possible in the dry season when there were no mosquitoes lurking about. It the rainy season, if the rain didn't wash you away, the mosquitoes would carry you away.

Chapter 33

BACK TO THE MIDDLE EAST (2010)

Twenty-five years after first planting our lives in Africa, and a mountain of challenging experiences now under our belts, we were sensing that God was whispering in our ears once again. That whispering began during our last year or so in Southern Sudan. We began to take notice of things that God was putting on our hearts. We now had a great group of church leaders that had some excellent training, were well equipped in church planting, and had been empowered to take the reins of the work that had begun. We had built an excellent coalition of churches from the States that was actively involved in several areas of service, such as drilling and maintaining wells, building schools and hospitals, leadership training, agricultural schemes, women's training programs, medical outreach into remote villages, and the oral Bible school we had begun. They would continue working there even when we left.

The past ten years had been spent in a land that was primarily an animistic-religions environment. What was predominately called the *Christian South* by most publications was far from the truth. Many of the early churches established in the south allowed the people to come to church on Sundays and carry on with their animistic tribal practices, which included witchcraft, among other practices. The rest of the week, with no condemnation of those practices, people pretty much carried on life with a number of gods in their lives. At one point I asked my local leaders how many witchdoctors there were in our village district. Though I had only met a few of them, they all told me there were over one hundred! Walking into that environment was very challenging. We often said that we were not beginning from the ground up, but rather we were in a basement and had to start from there by rebuilding the foundation of biblical truth with which we would build on.

Animism is the belief that objects, places, and creatures all possess a distinct spiritual essence. Potentially, animism perceives all things—animals, plants, rocks, rivers, weather systems, human handiwork, and sometimes even words—as animated and alive. The following made-up illustration should help.

Hundreds of years ago, there was a man who left his village in Sudan and headed to another one far away to see some relatives. It took many days to make the trip, and about halfway there the man ran out of food and water. It was in the very hot season, and the man was near to death when he crawled underneath a tree for some shade. As he rested propped up along the trunk of the tree, expecting to die, suddenly a piece of fruit from the tree dropped into his lap. The man opened the fruit and found it was juicy, so he ate more of them. It revived him enough to continue on with his journey. When he reached his destination, he told the village the story of the tree, as he also did when he returned to his home village. From that time forward, the tree was revered by his tribe and clan, and no one was ever allowed to cut one down. They worshiped the "god" in it from that day forward.

About one to two years into our work in the south, we discovered a book written by a man named Robert Blaschke, called, *Quest for Power*.[9] The purpose of his book is to provide Christians with a biblically sound approach for the communication of the gospel to animists in terms relevant to their worldview, culture, and language. One communication bridge that strikes into the core of animists' thinking is the revelation that they worship created things cursed by God, while at the same time not even acknowledging the existence of the almighty Creator, let alone worshiping Him. Part of Blaschke's book focuses on suggestions for the initial communication of the gospel to animists. Some of it describes a model developed for the training of barely literate church leaders in their traditional learning style in locations without a resident Bible school—what is commonly called "storying." This was essential in our area as we were predominantly using oral methods of Bible teaching. Since over half of the world's population understands only the non-Western way of thinking, this book was of great value to help both us as well as all of the teams that we brought out to work alongside us. We made it required reading for any team coming our way. One team leader that came out often actually bought a case of the books directly from the author.

Due to the uptick of the fighting in Darfur, there were now some Fur people migrating into our area of the south. They were mostly traders in the local market area in Rumbek, and we began a relationship with them very early on. Because they only spoke Arabic and not the local Dinka language, we really enjoyed talking with them. As we had been in the North for many years, we found we could really relate to

---

9. Robert Blaschke, *A Quest for Power* (Guardian Books, January 1, 2001).

them and the struggles they were encountering. We could see and feel God doing something in our hearts—drawing us back into working with the Arab peoples again.

Another clear sign was our health. When we started the work in the South, we were still young and fit and ready to tackle all that the South had in store for us. Ten years on, and the dirt and mud *roads*; the bouts of malaria; the living in a harsh environment without electricity; the constant acts of war that surrounded us daily; the snakes, scorpions, and other stinging insects—all these and more had begun to take a toll on us. When I was medevaced out to Nairobi during my last bout of malaria, our medical personnel informed me that our time in the South was nearing an end (they actually said it was over).

Each of these, and several other markers from God, suggested to us that He wanted us to begin a new work for Him. That is when the final whisper made its way to our ears, and God's affirmation was made clear: "Have I got a great place for you," came the invitation from a colleague working in the Middle East. Initially we understood that he was talking about working on an island off the coast of Africa, and we were all in. Well, that wasn't what he had in mind. Turns out he asked us about returning to the Middle East again. It had been about thirteen years since we were last there studying Arabic, and, to be honest, we were beginning to miss the place. Our Arabic had grown rusty while working in Southern Sudan, as very few people used it there. They mostly communicated in their tribal dialects, which numbered over two hundred. Official government offices were one of the few places where Arabic, as well as English, was still widely used, but we tried to avoid those offices every chance we got. So now we would need to take about a year to refresh our Arabic language skills and figure out the next steps to moving into our new country.

BACK TO THE MIDDLE EAST (2010)

We moved to Southern Jordan where there were far fewer English speakers in the country, and I began meeting with a man every day for about two to four hours. We would talk about anything that came to mind. Simple, casual conversations that ranged from airplanes to the weather. My vocabulary and pronunciation increased and improved daily. Kate was meeting with women in our apartment building and talking about life with them. About ten months in, we were feeling pretty confident that we were back where we needed to be linguistically, and we had found a job working with a company that I had worked with before that wanted to open up an office in Omari.* I made a couple of trips into the country to talk with some connections our company president had made, to scope out possible places to rent, and to meet some government officials who had invited us to participate in a large project in the capital city. It certainly appeared that God had a plan for our lives, and we could see it unfolding in those early days.

Chapter 34

OMARI

Our new country was nothing like Jordan, where we had spent three years of our lives and loved living. Even when making the decision to leave there and go where we were clearly being called, it was very hard. We had grown to love the place we were living and could see ourselves spending many years there. Kate was sure that living in that city was in the original conversations we had had with our supervisor, but he didn't seem to remember that part. One of the valuable parts of going back to Jordan was that it was a perfect middle-of-the-road spot for us. It was not as poor as our past country and not as wealthy as the one we were going to, so it made the change not so dramatic for us.

So off we went to start new work once again. This would be the third time we had been asked to start foundational work in our careers. Kate often refers to us as the company's designated guinea pigs. We informed our supervisor that we would give the company the next ten years of our lives to get things up and running, and then we would move on. As I write this, we are in year nine, just a few months before the big ten arrives. I'm continually reminding my boss of this fact. (Now, as I review this for the umpteenth time, we have already made the shift to another country.)

While we were still in Jordan, I decided to start a blog—for several reasons, one of which was to write things that I felt I would want to say yet realized would not be wise to put on the internet under my own name. Mostly just observations about what I was seeing in a very conservative environment, unlike any we had been in before. Sudan, to a degree, was quite closed to foreigners, but the people themselves were so incredibly kind and generous that the oppressions that came from the government were somehow lessened as one gathered and interacted with the Sudanese people on a normal, daily basis. It was not uncommon to be walking down a street and have a total stranger ask you into their home for a cup of tea or a cold drink. Our new country was not to be like that. In fact, over the decade we spent there we could count on one hand the number of homes we had been invited into. Our new society was certainly not like our previous ones.

We had done a good bit of research prior to moving to our new assignment. We were good friends with a couple that had pioneered working in this country about fifteen years before. We picked their brains as much as we could about everything we could think of. We realized it had been a decade since they had lived there and that they lived in the capital city and we would not be there, but they were immensely helpful in giving us some groundwork with which we could make some decisions. When we finally landed in the city that we would call home for the next decade, we met a wonderful young couple who worked for another company. Jim* and Ellie* would be our go-to advisors for the next several months as we navigated our new surroundings and the cultural nuances we were encountering. God had given to us the sweetest of welcoming gifts—a friendship that continues to this day. Even though they relocated to another country about a year after we arrived, by that time we had our feet wet and were wading waist high in the streams of our new culture.

Going from one of the poorest countries in the world at that time (and still to this day) to one that has a very high per capita for its citizens was quite a culture shock. We went from having no paved roads to smooth tarmac everywhere, no electricity to 24/7 power, water from a borehole to running city water, no place to purchase everyday items to a land that has more malls than we have been able to count, no buildings higher than one story (mostly made of mud and thatch) to high-rise buildings everywhere, people living in abject poverty earning about two dollars a day to people who went to restaurants and ate about a tenth of what was served and threw the rest away. The stark contrast was everywhere to see and experience.

The people we lived and worked with in Southern Sudan were lucky if they had three good shirts and two pairs of pants. If they had one good pair of shoes, they were fortunate. Very few had any money in a bank, as most of their wealth was in their cattle and flocks of goats. Now we had been catapulted into a land of immense wealth due to their vast oil reserves, which feeds the ever-growing world population with its hunger for industry and capital advancement. Even though Southern Sudan itself had proven reserves of this precious commodity, it has been continually strangled by the North in their attempts to get it to the world markets. It will probably be years in the future before any real change is seen in that newest nation in the world.

One of the first notable things about our new country was the driving. We went from a county where we knew every vehicle in the whole district of forty-three-thousand square miles to one where vehicles were piled on top of each other. One where we would see another vehicle on the road every half hour or so (every day or so in the early years) to one where they would fly by us going two hundred kilometers per hour. While drivers in both countries are not very good, at least you had plenty of time to get out of the way in Southern Sudan. At two hundred kilometers per hour, you have only a split second to make life and death decisions. Ten years later I still have not felt a peace about going out onto the roads each day. I actually wrote up a list of driving rules after being there for a while . . . .

Chapter 35

DRIVING

Driving here is not just a means of transport from one place to another; it's a social event. You talk on your phones, you work on business deals, you socialize with your friends, and, least of all, you pay attention to where you are going.

If you are bigger than the other guy, you have the right of way.

When you come into a traffic circle, look in every direction. If you think you have the right of way, you don't. The vehicle coming from the other side at a high rate of speed does.

If you think the vehicle to the right of you on a four-lane road can't turn left at the approaching turn-around or traffic light, think again. He can. And he will. If the vehicle has its left turn signal on, it means that he is turning left even though he's in the far right lane. So beware.

The shortest distance from point A to point B is *not* a straight line. You will need to go at least two miles out of your way to get where you want to go.

The road that was there yesterday may not be there tomorrow.

Traffic jams at midnight are the norm. Just more time to socialize.

Road rage is real and alive here. Since there are no traffic police doing their jobs (unless you consider drinking coffee all day long a job), you could be pulled out of your vehicle and smacked around by a crazy person with no repercussions (and yes, we have seen that happen).

You will be in accidents. Know the number for the traffic police for something serious. For most minor dings, you get out, yell a bit, make lots of arm movements, assess the damage, agree what to do on the spot, and move on. Do *not* let relatives of the driver come to "assist." You will be found guilty within two minutes, no matter what happened. If you are a foreigner, you are the guilty party—full stop.

Female drivers: there used to be plenty of old clichés about female drivers in America about sixty years ago. They are mostly true here today.

If there is a puddle in the road, a small pothole, or a speed bump, you can be assured that there will be an ensuing traffic jam. It is the commonly held belief that their vehicle will melt by touching water or disintegrate going over a bump in the road. Vehicles will back up miles for a bit of water in the road.

Lines for parking spaces are simply parking lot decorations. They mean nothing, except maybe that you are supposed to park your vehicle across them or center your vehicle on them, but certainly not between them. Lines on the roads are the same. Again, it is commonly believed that you drive down the middle of, as opposed to between, them.

DRIVING

Many drivers here drive like they are still on their camels in the desert. You direct your camel where you want to go and just go. You can turn anywhere you want, anytime you want, for any reason you want. That other vehicles are surrounding you and you are traveling at ninety miles per hour is of no consequence.

Don't let the other driver you are in an accident with say to you, "Let's just forget all this; the traffic police are taking too long to come." If he does, just stay and wait for the police. The alternative will be your being denied to leave the country when you are at the airport ready to go on your family holiday.

Never drive a vehicle without a properly working horn. The louder the better.

That "emergency" half-lane next to the center of the concrete road barrier is actually a passing lane for drivers who need to go thirty kilometers per hour over the limit. Be very wary.

Never, ever, never take your eyes off the road. That includes watching through every mirror your vehicle has at all times. Using your rearview mirror is just as valuable as looking ahead.

When you are in the left lane and see a vehicle flashing his lights at you from a mile back, move over quickly. He will pass you in the next ten seconds—whether you move over or not.

Do not leave your driveway or enter the roads without buckling your seatbelt. Vehicles can go just as fast on side roads as they can on the highways.

Remember, you have citizens from around the world driving on these roads. Most of them didn't drive before coming here and simply bought their license in a local *souk* (market).

If you see a ten-year-old driving on the road next to you, don't panic. His mom or grandfather needs to be someplace, and he's the only male left in the house to get them there. Just because you can only see his eyes doesn't mean he can't drive. . . .

Tips for remaining calm and peaceful behind the wheel of a vehicle: there are none that have worked so far. Praying before leaving, spiritual music playing, Bible verses pasted to the dashboard, praying while driving, singing hymns while driving, having a pastor in your vehicle—all have failed miserably.

Just one short story to illustrate some of the above. My wife and I had been in the city for less than two months and were driving down one of the main north-south roads where there were kilometers-long stretches without a place to turn around. I had moved over into the far-left lane as I approached one of those scarce turnarounds, when all of a sudden, I see the flashing lights in my rearview mirror. Because I needed to turn left in the next few seconds, I just ignored the driver and kept going. Big mistake. When I didn't move, he pulled up alongside of us, gestured wildly at me, and promptly jerked his low-slung sedan into the side of my SUV. Thankfully I was holding the steering wheel tightly and avoided crashing into the foot-high curbs on the median. The driver of that vehicle then sped off at an exceedingly high speed. Needless to say, my wife and I were shaken by the incident.

A few nights later we were having our twenty-something neighbors over for dinner, and we recounted the affair to them. They just started to laugh. Then they proceeded to tell us how common that was and about some of the road rage vehicle battles they had had. After they were finished with their stories, we realized how *minor* ours had been!

Chapter 36

STARTING OUT . . . AGAIN

Prior to visiting Omari with Kate, I made two or three trips in with representatives of our company. We were meeting people who were involved with the massive project we were invited to be a part of with the government, as well as others who were involved with programs similar to what we wanted to execute in-country. We needed some local partners who had shared interests and were willing to work in concert with us to bring a much-needed upgrade to our sector of the society. We weren't sure how we would find them, but God had that one under control.

It didn't take long for us to fit into the new assignment. We began meeting people from our first week in the country. Having previously worked in the Arab world, we knew that things would move slowly, but we were confident that God was leading us every step of the way. Outwardly, people were quite friendly and eager to engage with us. The number of coffee shops, restaurants, and office meetings we had was quite large in those early days. Yet as I mentioned earlier, that is usually where the boundaries for relationships ended. One exception was a group of young men who were just starting a company similar to the international one we worked for. There were a lot of shared interests, thoughts, and dreams that honestly made us a *match made in heaven*. We had worked with Arabs in other countries before without many issues, so we were pretty sure we would be able to work alongside these young men who truly had a passion for their start-up.

We did and are still doing so to this day. Fine young men whom we have come to know, as well as their families and friends. We have been there for births, weddings, deaths, Eid celebrations, Thanksgiving meals in our home, and a host of other joyous times together. I can say for certain that God put them into our lives to be an encouragement all the years we lived there. The insights into the culture that they provided us and their unfailing support when others said things about us that were not accurate, produced an enduring friendship that will last far into the future.

From the beginning of this relationship, we made it clear that we were believers in the Jesus of the Bible. They, too, knew of Jesus, but in a far different way than we do. Their understanding is from the Koranic perspective that equates Jesus as just another prophet like Moses, Elijah, or Abraham. They understand that He lived a sinless life, was born of a virgin, and had powers that no other person has ever had. But the cross, and the belief that Jesus is the Son of God, is their stumbling block. Understanding the love of God for humanity through the death of His Son is something they still have an exceedingly difficult time grasping. And though we had, and continue to have, numerous conversations with each of them, they are still grounded in their Islamic faith. They are continually being interceded for by numerous believers, and we continue to hold on to the hope that is within us that He will reveal His true self to them one day.

STARTING OUT... AGAIN

It was on one of these first trips in that I had a *vision*, actually a request to God, for help. The meetings we had been involved with over the previous days were all completed, and my colleagues had already taken their flights out to the countries where they lived. My flight back to Jordan was about a day later. I decided to do some exploring around the city and wound up on the shoreline of the sea. There was nothing there at that time other than some large boulders and a bunch of sea birds cruising around. As I sat there in conversation with God, we talked about what I had seen and observed over the past week. I reflected on the fact that a huge majority of the population in this country were under the age of thirty. With Kate and I being almost twice that age, I recognized that we were going to need an army of teammates who would be able to relate culturally with the local youth. I sat there on one of those rocks, and as I watched the waves continuously roll in off the sea, I asked God to provide waves of young men and women to come to those shores with a heart to share truth in a land of darkness.

As the years went by, we watched His faithfulness in providing answers to that cry, and by the time we left a decade later, there were more than sixty people thirty years old and under living in that city who were dedicated to proclaiming truth and living out their faith. That is an answered prayer that we will always be grateful for until the day we meet the Lord in heaven. And it was not only my prayer but many who served for years in the country before us. And even a multitude who never set foot in the land yet who continually prayed for it.

I knew I would not remember all the ways that we saw the Master at work there, so putting down words and stories was my way of being able to look back at His goodness. I'm going to include very few of these here, with some alterations, to give you a feel of how amazing it was to watch God work

NOT QUITE FINISHED

with so little input from us. Quite different from other places that we had served.

Chapter 37

BLOG POSTS

Been doing a lot of introspective thinking the past several weeks. I guess that tends to happen when one is preparing to leave behind familiar (and jaw-droppingly beautiful) surroundings for something less than that. I told a story to a friend of mine this past week about walking down into town one day not long ago. I was sauntering along having this great conversation with God—most of it out loud—about how much my wife and I really loved living where we do now (and for the next few weeks).

Perhaps I was having some remorseful feelings at having to once again pack up a household, move to another strange place, and start all over again. After all, we are not talking about a move from one city to another or one state to another, where everyone speaks English, and the sports are baseball, basketball, and football. No, this is, as usual for us, from one country to another where the spoken language is the second hardest in the world, and the dialects are different in each country (Arabic), and the sports are soccer, sand dune riding, and . . . more soccer—with a bit of falconry thrown in. We know almost no one in the new country other than our new landlord with whom we had a brief time with over a cup of tea and some dates. Once again, we are at ground zero.

Now there are some great advantages to being in this position. We get to meet and befriend some very interesting and fascinating people from another culture. We talk with them in their own language, eat in their homes, attend weddings and social gatherings with their families, and often end up with lifetime friendships that span the continents. Some of what we don't have are family nearby (though Skype has greatly helped with this), next door neighbor "friends for years," nesting in one abode for more than a few years at a time, or big Thanksgiving Day dinners complete with football games.

So, as God and I were talking and reminiscing over the past year, He reminded me of a little whisper that He breathed to me and my wife when we first arrived here: I know you need some time to refresh yourselves from the past years of challenging service, so these coming months are a little gift from me. Oh, and what an amazing refreshment and redirecting of my soul it has been. To wake up each new morning as the sun spreads its rays from one mountain range to the other, and to sit on our verandah many evenings and see His stunning creation in this part of the world, is a gift that will always be remembered. Now it's time to move on to the tasks ahead of us in this new season of service. Sadness, a little bit excitement, much more confidence—at the max.

***

Woke up early this morning, very early. As my mind started cranking up, I tried to lay in bed listening to Matt Boswell on my iPod, hoping that I would soon fall back into restful slumber. But alas, after an entire album of praise, here I sit. I could blame it on jet lag, which could be a part of it, but the deep-down root is that I started thinking about, Where is he?—*the "he" being the person to whom God's spirit has been speaking to about me.* Where does he live? What kind of family does he come from? How many children does he have? How long has he been looking for me? How did he come to know the God I love?

These and many more questions are even now racing through the network of my mind and heart as my wife and I look forward to our impending trip next week. It's to be a time of exploration—looking for housing, meeting influential people, practicing the local dialect, locating a vehicle, meeting with government officials about visa issues, trying to get a business endeavor cranked up, etc. But most of all, I will be searching for him. *Or should I say, being available for him to find me. It may not happen that soon, but I would be overjoyed if it did. We certainly have many people interceding for this one purpose.*

I wonder what his dream will look like . . . I'm fairly certain that he has, or will have, some kind of vision telling him that I exist and that I'm looking for him. Something in his heart will be stirring, a strange sensation of anticipation and wonderment that is the twin of my own heart's quaking. The knowing that something good, and bold, and challenging, and on the cusp of being big, is about to happen. Something that tells you that the Spirit is in control, and you are simply along for the ride.

Over the past few months I have heard the enemy's voice whispering to me quite a bit: This challenge is too big for you. You don't know what you are doing. Your language skills are never going to cut it for this assignment. Where you live now is really comfortable; do you really want to move yet again? You're too old to be taking on this type of challenge. This is a fairly dangerous place to go and live. *It seems like the doubts keep coming in waves. It's a good thing that I have the peace that passes all understanding for this season of life. My hope is built on nothing less than His blood and righteousness. Thank you, Matt, for reminding me of that fact this early morning.*

***

During this first trip in with Kate, we had what turned out to be the first of many amazing experiences over the years.

Last night my wife and I had an incredible evening digging into the Word with a local family of believers. We were joined by others from Europe and the Middle East in what, for me, was a feast. I recalled the words of the two men who were walking along the Emmaus road and encountered the Word incarnate and later recalled, "Didn't our hearts leap with joy?" I had that same feeling last night as we sat around a small room and dug into the riches that help guide our daily lives. The focus was on the second chapter of the second letter to Timothy. Most of the evening was conducted in Arabic, so we were certainly stretched in that respect. There were a few times when we had to pause for some interpreting assistance, though I actually did some interpreting myself for another person there who did not know Arabic at all.

While we are not sure yet if these are the people of peace that we have been praying for, they certainly did bring great joy to us for an evening. We are hoping to be with them one more time before we return to home and then continue on with them once we plant ourselves in the land in the near future.

Our time here has been very beneficial as far as home hunting and multitudes of meetings with businesspeople, lawyers, and realtors, but without a doubt the reason we were here this time was to meet this family and share bread with them. As we were driving home last night, I was thinking, Wow, this is what it's all about. And it is.

***

I've never struggled to wake up when the sun peaks over the eastern horizon. For as long as I can remember, getting up early has been a part of my daily routine. Still is somewhat, but the past few weeks I have really been struggling. I think to myself, Maybe it's the heat? *Naw*, I've been living in over one-hundred-degree temperatures for too many years for that to reason out. Maybe it's just that I'm getting older? That's a fairly lame excuse considering the good physical shape that the Master has blessed me with all of my life. Possibly the stress of moving, yet again, to unfamiliar surroundings with few friends in place? Perhaps, but since we have been down that road over a dozen times the past couple of decades, I can't see that one as holding much water (or sand).

Right about now, I'm pretty confident that this struggle is a straightforward spiritual warfare battle. My precious morning time is when I dig into the Word and seek new treasures every day that will help sustain me in my spiritual walk. Waking up unrefreshed is making those times very challenging. Thankfully the lifetime routine has been pretty well established, but the joy is now diminished somewhat. And that is something that is not pleasant. My sleep has been poor for the first time in my life, and waking up groggy is something that, until now, has been reserved for the infrequent sicknesses I have endured during my life.

A couple of weeks ago, in the quiet of a morning, I walked all around our new flat, room by room, and prayed. I asked for special blessings on each one—the majlis (a large sitting room for Arab men to gather in) for bringing people together to fellowship, the kitchen/dining room for healthy food and good relationships, the office for work that will be a blessing to the Master, the guest bedroom for weary travelers to find rest, the *master bedroom for a place of rest and intimacy with my wife, the bathrooms for . . . yeah. For the whole of the house, I prayed for any lurking demonic presences of the past to be removed, that the work of the Holy Spirit might flourish in all who walk through our doors and enjoy the hospitality of what God has lent to us for a season.*

Maybe that made the enemy mad at me. I don't know. But I know that for the past few weeks now, my wife and I have really been feeling the conflict that comes when engaged in spiritual battle. Bickering instead of encouraging, walking separately instead of together, complaining instead of praising—all clear signs that the enemy in sneaking into our midst where we don't want him. The good thing is that we are aware of this and are fighting back. The tough part is that when one is constantly fatigued, that battle is even harder. Again, I'm sure the enemy has his hand in that. So please join us as we battle through this season and ask that we will be victorious for our King and that glory will come to Him and His purposes for our lives will be clear.

***

So, it's 10:45 p.m., and there is a knock at our door. My wife and I are watching a movie after getting home from an evening of walking around a couple of malls, looking for things we needed. Did a lot of people watching—black tents for women, white-pressed dishdashas for the men. The styles just don't ever seem to change here. When I first arrived here, I was pretty amazed at how quickly the landscape of boring black just kind of faded into the background and went practically unnoticed.

Then tonight, as I was once again studiously observing the culture and joining in at a local coffee establishment at the mall, I realized how tired I am of seeing this field of unending black. Lots of mixed emotions racing through my mind. By now we are well aware of both sides of the debate about the abayas—some women like wearing them while others feel stifled in them. Since I don't have to wear one, I really don't have much to say on that either way, but it doesn't alter the fact that to my eyes, it's really boring and drab to see a sea of black everywhere I go, every day.

So, after the knock at the door came the invitation, from a black tent, for my wife to come to a party. Of course she says, "OK," and quickly puts on makeup and very nice party clothes. That is one of the quirky things about the culture here—underneath those black tents are women who are dressed in the latest fashions from Milan, Paris, and New York. When women go to parties, they are dressed to the nines, as my parents used to say.

If someone told me a couple of years ago that we would be going "out" after 10 p.m., I would just have laughed . . . or cried. But one does what one needs to do to be with the people one is called to be with, no matter the time of day or night. Now if only this culture would recognize that the Creator created all those beautiful colors of the rainbow for the human eye to see and not to be shrouded in black, I think I would be happier. And my eyes would be grateful. . . .

***

I recently read something that talked about how Paul, near the end of his life here on this planet, reiterated and expressed how the most important thing in his life was knowing Christ. After years and years of what appears to be a very faith-filled ministry, he did not expound on planting more churches, making more disciples, or writing profound letters to the masses; rather, he was zeroed in on what he realized mattered most—knowing the Master in a deeper, more intimate way.

It's not that I haven't heard or read this before, but I guess this caught my attention now more than ever before as I read the wisdom of this insight of "being near the end of his ministry." My wife and I have lived overseas for about three decades or so now. While in faith we are looking forward to many more years of faithful service, we are also realists. There are some days when I get up and I wonder, Where in the world did that ache come from? *Or other mornings when I wonder why I feel miserable after only getting four or five hours of sleep. Even my daily afternoon siestas don't seem to be providing me with the energy I usually get. Some of that may be psychological, knowing that the next four to five months will see temperatures above one hundred every day. That's what I keep telling myself anyway.*

Both of us have been abundantly blessed with amazing health all of our lives, both physically and spiritually. There have been plenty of highs and lows. There have been dark nights of the soul and views from the mountain tops. There have been jumps out of airplanes and weeks of bed-ridden malaria. There have been moments of seeing His awesome grace at work and days of wondering, Where did He go? Through it all, it has been a journey in search of knowing Him on a deeper level, all with the goal of finishing strong.

"Having the mind of the Master"—does He curse the driver that just swerved in front of me? Does He get angry when government offices continually send us in circles while we try to work within their regulations? Does He get discouraged when I can't communicate adequately with someone in their first language, even though I've studied for years on end? Does He have a smile on His face when I watch injustices imposed on females in this society? Oh my, I could go on and on in the multitude of ways that I feel like I do not live up to 1 Corinthians 2:16. All I can say is that it sure is a good thing that I live on this earth by His grace and that He has a character of a loving Father who understands that I continually try to be pleasing to Him, and at the same time I am weak in nature.

It's a lifelong journey and one that I'm not willing to give up on—even in my failures.

***

Uncertain, unknown, perils, fearful, full of panic, worrisome, *and* hyped up *are all words to describe the gamut of emotions and decision-making that is going on in the world today. The latest virus that affects human beings to enter our world has really come with a splash and a* bang. *The news media are all over it, and that is both good and bad. Having the discernment to understand all that has been filling the airways and the internet has been a real challenge. Just two days ago I saw an article that compared the four past viruses of recent memory and the amount of worldwide press that each one got. MERS, SARS, Ebola, and Spanish Flu all combined for a minuscule fraction of what has been out there on this coronavirus. Having read through many of them to get a read on this pandemic, I have discerned that accurate information is challenging to come by. And unfortunately, much of it is panic inciting in nature.*

There seems to be a growing consensus that this is one to be taken seriously, especially by the elderly population. Until now, several months from its inception, no children are reported to have died as a direct result of the virus. Apparently they could be carriers, but they have some sort of immunity.

What is interesting to me in all of this is the very small amount of press or chatter that is talking about the sovereignty of God. There is a lot of talk going on about "what can we do" to stem the tide or to stop this thing, but little about God being the one who is the knower of all the information about the virus. I would posit that one question we believers should be asking ourselves is, What does God expect of me during this worldwide pandemic? *There is a wonderful quote from Martin Luther written during the time of the plague in Europe. It goes like this:*

Very well, by God's decree the enemy has sent us poison and deadly offal. Therefore, I shall ask God mercifully to protect us. Then I shall fumigate, help purify the air, administer medicine, and take it. I shall avoid places and persons where my presence is not needed in order not to become contaminated and thus perchance infect and pollute others, and so cause their death as a result of my negligence. If God should wish to take me, he will surely find me, and I have done what he has expected of me and so I am not responsible for either my own death or the death of others. If my neighbor needs me, however, I shall not avoid place or person but will go freely, as stated above. See, this is such a God-fearing faith because it is neither brash nor foolhardy and does not tempt God.[10]

This quote is part of a long article that Luther wrote concerning a Christian's response to the deadly plague that was rampaging through Europe centuries ago. I thought it about sums up what my response should be during this crisis— being the fragrance of God at a time of great worldwide, and, bringing it home, community need. I have responsibilities to those around me—my wife, my children, my teammates, my neighbors, and those who live in the same location as me. That responsibility today includes not gathering in large groups of people, not shaking hands in a culture where that is so

---

10. Martin Luther, Luther's Works, Vol 43: Devotional Writings II, ed. Jaroslav Jan Pelican, Hilton C. Oswald, and Helmut T. Lehmann, vol 43 (Philadelphia: Fortress Press, 1999), 119–38.

very important, not going outside when I may find myself with a fever or coughing, or failing to wash my hands when I have been engaged with the outside world. It also includes offering to go get groceries for my elderly neighbor, going to a pharmacy to bring medicine for the woman with four kids in her flat, taking care of my neighbors' plants while they are out of the country, or even taking someone to the hospital who is sick with what appears to be the dreaded virus.

There is no room for panic in the sovereignty of God. There is only room for responsibility. My hope is that I will look back on these challenging months a few years from now and be able to recognize that the aroma I sent up to heaven was one that found favor with God.

***

During these days of Covid, I have learned one thing for sure. I would have made a lousy POW. I have lived overseas for the past three decades, so one would think that I would be used to different levels of uncomfortable. I have lived in the bush with some of the poorest of Africa's poor and have lived on the edge of two deserts. I have survived living ten years in one of the worst places on this planet for incurable and unknown diseases. I've even lived among SARS, dengue fever, and malaria-riddled zones and have come out on the other end fairly unscathed. Yet this Corona thing is really messing with me.

As I woke up this morning from more than two months of lock-down curfew, I was greeted with the reality of a new five-day total curfew. No one allowed outside, no travel, no groceries (unless ordered as delivery), nada. Much of the rest of the world has already begun to reopen after the brunt of the virus has passed through. But here, we are locking down even more severely. That is playing with the mind. Just yesterday I had a conversation with a friend in the States and found myself being jealous of the freedoms of movement that he was experiencing. He was talking about going here and there, doing this and that, while I just listened with envy.

Then it hit me again. It's not the first time during this season, but this one had an even more forceful punch to it. As I listened to my mind grumble about being in yet another, even more severe curfew situation, my thoughts were immediately transported to all the people who have been POWs during a war. Or political prisoners of a rogue state. Or refugees in a resettlement camp that is not in their own country. Oh my. Even as I write this, I am so convicted of harboring my thoughts of "capture." When I can still cook my own food from my well-stocked pantry, drink clean, cold water from my fridge, read books when I want, go up on my roof and exercise, talk with my neighbors (at a safe distance), check out news on the internet, watch Netflix, or enjoy my air-conditioned flat—I feel ashamed at the selfish thoughts I have of being contained for a mere five days.

Yet there it is, nagging at me. Complaining about how long it's been since I could freely go out to have coffee with a friend, or walk along the beach, or take a swim at my gym. And as I look at the future according to government press *releases here, it appears that there is going to be about three more months of these curtailed restrictions in place. How am I going to hang in there that long? Physically, I'm fine. Mentally and emotionally, I'm not so sure. I'm pretty sure I would have made a terrible POW. And then, there it is again . . . Paul in prison, in chains, no lighting other than perhaps an oil lamp, rats scampering everywhere, cold, dank, lonely. And what do we see him recorded as doing? Singing and praising God! What? How? Oh Lord, please give me that fortitude and mental strength to be like that.*

And there are untold other stories quite similar to Paul's. People who hid in caves for years on deserted islands, ones that endured years as kidnapped captives in isolation, or ones who walked for months with little or no food to avoid war. And here I am. Just five days. Eating. Reading and writing. Snugly sitting in a cushioned chair. A loving wife at my side. Sleeping in a comfortable bed. Feeling pretty shamed right now for even having the thoughts I had when I woke up. May the God who created all things give comfort to the truly needy in these days. I am certainly not one of them.

Chapter 38

THREE MEN

Prior to even going into Omari, I had been praying for months for the Master to allow me to meet up with the person who was waiting for me in there. That didn't take long as we very quickly met Alex* and his family. Within a few short weeks we began meeting with all of them on a weekly basis at the home of a dear friend of ours. Our friend was a natural Arabic speaker, so he and his family were always able to help us out when we got into language trouble. Alex had an amazing faith journey that I will only briefly cover here.

He was a *muezzin* (one who announces the call to prayer) until he began watching a church channel in a private room in his home. It was a preacher from Egypt whose words caught his heart and changed his course of life forever. After a lengthy period of faithfully watching and then giving his heart to Jesus, he decided he needed to go to Egypt, find this church he had been watching on TV, and get some discipleship from that pastor. So he sold his house and land, left his family with other family members, and went off to

Egypt. He walked around the city for three days until he found the church he had only seen on TV. He spent the next three months or so being discipled there and then came back to Omari. He promptly led his family to faith in Jesus, and shortly later we met up.

We spent months meeting together, until one evening I seem to have gotten too aggressive in my charge to be expressive of their faith to their neighbors and friends. The night ended with loud voices expressing that I didn't understand what it was like being a believer in Omari, and that they could lose their lives for doing what I had suggested. I literally didn't see Alex for another eight months. Then, at a football event one day, up walks Alex, along with a friend that I knew was also a believer. After the unique cultural greetings were shared, he proceeded to tell me all that God had done in his life the past months—and it was a lot! He started a group in his home studying the Word; his daughters, who were the angriest with us, had led someone to faith; and his wife was teaching some of the foreign wives how to cook local food as well as teaching them spiritual dialogue in Arabic. I was overjoyed because I thought I had destroyed a work that God had begun and was feeling very depressed about it.

Within a couple of years, he was deported from the country—though not for being a believer. He has since been in several other countries serving the King and being faithful to his calling.

I was somewhat upset that God had allowed this man to leave after all the time we had spent with him, but I quickly began asking Him to provide me with another person to disciple. That came about very quickly as Andrew* appeared on the radar.

Three years of myself, my wife, and a couple of our teammates all having a hand in the faith walk of Andrew. Way too many stories to put down here but perhaps a couple that should be told. At the time of meeting him, Andrew had

THREE MEN

recently met a young lady, Pricilla,* who was a believer. Her faith was not all that strong simply because she didn't have the people in her life that could help her grow, and Andrew wasn't quite there yet.

We started out by studying the book of Acts each week; I think it took us almost three years to get through it. My team and I had the inclination that Andrew was the guy who would be planting the first church in the city that we lived in, thus the book of Acts. A whole lot more came out of that study time than we could ever have imagined. A baptism, a PhD in missions, a lifelong friendship, leadership in a church, and so much more.

One of the *lighter side* stories was when we gathered each week in our homes, sometimes Pricilla would join us (she sometimes had to work in the evenings). When we started, we would read a passage from Acts and then ask Andrew to tell the story in his own words. It was often humorous as he would recall what he had seen in one of the films about Jesus as opposed to what we had just read. However, when Pricilla was there and was asked to tell the story, she would repeat it almost verbatim, including any and all named characters in the story. We gave Andrew a hard time about this.

So, after three years of mentoring and discipling and feeling like we were ready for the next phase of our work to grow, Andrew came to us and said, "I'm leaving to join the military" (in another country). Each of us freaked out and tried over and over to talk him out of it, and I even had some anger in me with the Lord over it. When the day came and he left the country, I put my gloves on and got into the ring with the Master. It didn't go well. I was a lot like Job in not understanding God's master plan and was terribly humbled over the next months. Long story short, Andrew only lasted a few weeks in the military when he realized that his plan for life was not his Master's plan for his life. He had already started working on his master's degree in missions when he left, and he quickly realized that that was the plan God wanted him to pursue. He obtained both his master's as well as his PhD and is now the leader of a church in another country.

The final young man, Malcom,* was God's present to me for having taken away the other two young men that I had buried myself in. And until this very day, Malcom and I communicate at least every week, and often more.

When I first met Malcom, I was of the understanding that he was already a believer and wanted to befriend someone who could help him better understand who Jesus was. That first hot and humid evening when we went for a long walk along the beach, I had him tell me the story of his faith walk, and I didn't discern anything to indicate that he was *not* a believer. (It could have been my language deficiency.) We spent the next year and a half meeting in our home and digging deep into the Word. Then one day he asked me if I would baptize him, to which I readily agreed. We had a secure place where there was a pool that we had used before, and I was humbled to be able to perform this ceremony.

Now in the Arab world that we had been a part of, when a person becomes a believer and is preparing to be baptized, they share their faith walk with all who are present at the ceremony. Sometimes it's in a church, sometimes it's rather private with only friends around as witnesses. They are always quite lengthy as the one being dunked shares their *whole* story, unlike the Western world where usually only a few words come from the mouth of the one being dunked. This was the latter of those (private), but it revealed something that I never knew. About ten to fifteen minutes in, I hear Malcom share that until he met me, he was not a believer. It was during our many nights together that at some point he made the decision to turn his life over to Jesus. I never even knew. And he currently lives in that realm of growing every day, closer to his Master, through some very challenging times, and some sweet ones.

I have joined him in both joys and deep sorrows as he has followed the Lord. Thankfully there have been others who have helped me along the way. Andrew has been one of those, giving Malcom great cultural advice on dealing with issues he was facing. And there were other teammates that were closer to Malcom's age that also were a key element as he walked in the light for the first time. Recently, as my wife and I traveled overseas to a country where we had never been before, Malcom came and joined us. It had been three years since we had seen each other, and we shared some very sweet time talking about Kingdom work.

Chapter 39

CLOSING OUT

Over the years we spent in Omari, we were able to develop a team of young professional people gifted in their fields and with a heart to teach truth at every opportunity given to them. We had begun branching out into different fields of business, coffee being one of them, and were excited and anticipatory at what the future held. Little did we know that Covid was what was in its hands. Within a year the team looked very different. During the lockdown, we only had ourselves and one other young lady from our team who stayed behind. The others wound up in different locations on both sides of the pond.

One of the benefits of being isolated there was an opportunity that I and a colleague from another team uncovered. At that time, travel was strictly prohibited with hefty fines ($1,000) for anyone caught outside without permission from the government. After a couple of months of lockdown, the two of us decided that on Tuesday of each week, we would drive through a selected *mantika* (neighborhood) and just pray as we drove through the streets. The streets were pretty much like a normal Friday morning—totally empty. We could drive at ease and stop pretty much anywhere we felt like to pray. We got a paper map of the city and divided up the mantikas. In a city of millions, we knew this was going to take some time, but we were up for the task, and Covid provided the time. We had a yellow highlighter to demarcate the areas that we prayed through. Prior to Kate and me leaving the country, we had prayed through more than half of the city. We left the remaining half in the hands of the new team leaders.

We saw some amazing answers to those prayers—sometimes quite quickly. One day when we were driving in a mantika, we saw many women, so we decided to pray for the women believers in the city (there were very few of them). We knew that in the Bible, women have a very key role in the spreading and growth of the gospel. Within a week, we heard a story of a woman who told a colleague that she was leading a group of six other ladies in studying the Bible.

One time we prayed for a work to be started in a particular mantika, and within a few days we heard that there was a believer living in that area now!

One day as we passed by numerous coffee shops, we prayed for them to be hubs for people to be sharing the truth about God and what He has done for the people of this country.

Those stories kept coming. There will never be anyone able to tell me that prayer is a waste of time or that it doesn't work.

Well, that decade of service came to a close. By God's grace we left behind new team leaders whom we had the privilege of mentoring for several years. They are just the right age and fit into the culture there perfectly. They will do a much better job than we did, as they build on the foundations that have been laid. They have already begun adding to the team we left behind, and we are super excited when we get updates from them, expounding on the new paths they are working in.

The writing was on the wall, and the voice of the Master made it clear that it was our time to move on to new frontiers. We needed to find the place that the Master had already designated for us to close out our *career* overseas service. Several options were presented, but when the Capestan option popped up, we both had a peace in our beings that this was the one. It would allow both of us to be actively involved in a team with the gifts and talents that God had given us. It has truly been a blessing. I have spent time mentoring many of the young men on that team, and Kate has spent most of her time working with the finances of the NGO we worked with.

The quite large team was filled with mostly first-termers who were in a stimulating and demanding environment. Out of necessity, the team leader wore more hats than he probably should have, and the political and cultural climates made for continuous unsteadiness. With a few missiles popping in here and there, and bad guys running around in the mountains, it made for a lively living situation. The team leader and his wife have done an excellent job of navigating all of the above and more, and now they have a solid team that is branching out into fields unknown in Capestan. They have given grace-filled leadership that has led to a very exciting time for everyone.

One of the very major requirements we put forth for our changing assignments was that we no longer wanted to be in leadership roles—no more decision making, no more reports to fill out, no computer time, no more financial responsibilities, no more team members to keep track of, no more . . . yeah, you get the idea. I just wanted to sit around in coffee shops, talking with people about Jesus. It turned out to be a variation of that. I don't meet with a lot of the local Arabs there, but I do meet with most of the male team members, as well as others, and we talk about our relationship with Jesus a lot. You see, God had a plan that I had not fully envisioned, and it is one that I have fully embraced and am loving. God never ceases to amaze me in that He knows me better than I know myself.

Chapter 40

PERSEVERANCE AND GRATEFULNESS

That first year in Southern Sudan was spellbinding and enthralling. Whether walking, riding a bicycle, or zipping through the bush on my motorcycle or 4-wheeler, God always had something unique in store for me and those that I worked with. Having never been in an environment quite like that before—living and working with people who still lived much like they did centuries ago, not knowing the local language, and trying my very best to listen to God's gentle whisper (and Him sometimes reprimanding me) as He led us along His paths of service—was at different times demanding, stimulating, stretching, joyful, and taxing. I don't ever remember a time when the thought entered our minds that it was too much for us. It was just simply what He had prepared us for.

During the second year, after having done as much due diligence as we could, we began planting churches. The first one was about a ten-minute walk from our compound. It started out well but never did grow the way we thought it would. I was perplexed, but there was a lot I didn't know. About seven or eight years later, as I was having a friendly chat with Abraham, one of the key evangelists working along-side us, he casually expounded on that first church plant. During the first year, the church setting (wooded pole pews, under a mango tree) was destroyed three different times by people in the community that didn't want it there. I only saw the damage once, and it was quickly explained to me something about vandals. The other times I knew nothing about. Now, as I sat there with Abraham, he unfolded how he and the other leaders of our church planting team were terrified to tell me of what really was going on, all because they feared I would then leave that work and go somewhere else.

At that early point, they did not understand the calling that the Master had put on our lives. They hadn't yet unpacked the stories of Paul, Barnabas, and others, and all that they endured to bring the gospel into unreached areas. As the years went on and on, the young leaders saw that we didn't flee just because of tribal fighting in the area, or in opposition to our churches from other established churches nearby, or having malaria several times, or living in safari tents for many years, or witchdoctors in the area putting curses on us, or. . . .

It took them years before they had the courage to tell me the story of that first plant. By that time, they knew what it was going to take to be committed servants of the Most High. They had seen it lived out by us and others who walked alongside us. They are still there today, still walking and biking those bush paths, still proclaiming the name that is above all names, and still suffering setbacks on a regular basis. But they are not giving up.

To God be the glory.

PERSEVERANCE AND GRATEFULNESS

Then Jesus said to his disciples, "The harvest is great, but the workers are few. So pray to the Lord who is in charge of the harvest; ask him to send more workers into his fields" (Luke 10:2).

www.ingramcontent.com/pod-product-compliance
Lightning Source LLC
Chambersburg PA
CBHW060508090426
42735CB00011B/2145